Bc

What a Savior!

What a Savior!

W. A. Criswell

"Nothing but the blood of Jesus" might well be the theme song of W.A. Criswell, pastor of the First Baptist Church, Dallas, Texas. He has preached the gospel of redemption through Christ's blood for fifty years.

WHAT A SAVIOR! consists of nineteen impassioned messages from the heart of this pastor/pulpiteer. Some of his chapter titles are: The Doctrine of Total Depravity, The Unpardonable Sin, The Blood of Christ, The Crimson Flow, Types of Calvary, The Shadow of the Cross, Behold the Lamb of God, What Shall I Do with Jesus?, and the Cross and the Crown, among others.

These messages will cause you to appreciate all the more what Jesus Christ has done through his atoning death. If you are a Christian, you will want to draw closer to Christ. If not, you will want to embrace him as your Savior . . . and you'll exclaim, WHAT A SAVIOR!

What a Savior!

W. A. Criswell

Broadman Press
Nashville, Tennessee

4251–55

ISBN: 0-8054-5155-2

Dewey Decimal Classification: 232

Subject Headings: JESUS CHRIST//ATONEMENT//SALVATION

Library of Congress Catalog Card Number: 77–082399

Printed in the United States of America

TO

OUR SENIOR ADULTS

who loved us enough
to teach us all about Jesus
and whose debtors we are forever.

Unless otherwise noted, all Scripture quotations are taken from the King James Version of the Bible.

Preface

The chapters in this book are preached sermons. They were delivered to the live audiences of the First Baptist Church in Dallas, and they were wonderfully blessed in their delivery. God gave us many souls. They are not written-out, theological treatises on the death of Christ. They are burning messages from the heart of a pastor to the hearts of the people who were and are hungry to hear the good news of our salvation in Christ Jesus.

There is a vast, immeasurable difference between a treatise and a sermon, between something written out and something delivered in the heat and fury of the pulpit. A sermon can be written out and can be delivered with great and telling effect by the writer's reading it to the people. Some of the greatest preachers of all time have carefully written out their sermons and have read them in the pulpit. But somehow it has always seemed to me that the fire and the flame which accompany the messenger from God, when he speaks with unction from heaven, are not nearly so apparent in the man who has his face in a manuscript as in a man who has his face toward his people and who is speaking to them heart to heart, soul to soul, eye to eye. Preaching will always mean to me the delivery of a burning message from a flaming heart to people who are intently and eagerly listening to the oracles of God. Preaching is a man in a pulpit surrounded by people who are listening with hungry hearts to the man who is delivering a message from heaven. Writing concerns a man at a desk in a study surrounded by books in a library.

These are just my own personal thoughts about preaching. To me, it is wonderful to see a man with just a Bible in his hand, after he has studied it and prayed over it, standing before the congregation to deliver his message in the power and unction of God.

In this sense and in this definition the chapters of this book are sermons. They were taken down stenographically and have been reproduced as they were delivered from the tapes.

May the Lord as graciously and as wondrously bless them to the eyes of the readers as he blessed them to the ears and the hearts of the congregation who first heard them.

W. A. CRISWELL

Dallas, Texas

Contents

PART 1
Sin—Our Condemnation

As it is written, There is none righteous, no, not one:

There is none that understandeth, there is none that seeketh after God.

They are all gone out of the way, they are together become unprofitable: there is none that doeth good, no, not one.

Their throat is an open sepulchre; with their tongues they have used deceit; the poison of asps is under their lips:

Whose mouth is full of cursing and bitterness:

Their feet are swift to shed blood:

Destruction and misery are in their ways:

And the way of peace have they not known:

There is no fear of God before their eyes.

Now we know that what things soever the law saith, it saith to them who are under the law: that every mouth may be stopped, and all the world may become guilty before God (Rom. 3:10–19).

In Evil Long I Took Delight

In evil long I took delight,
Unawed by shame or fear,
Till a new object struck my sight,
And stopped my wild career.

I saw One hanging on a tree,
In agonies and blood,
Who fixed His languid eyes on me,
As near His cross I stood.

Sure never till my latest breath
Can I forget that look:
It seemed to charge me with His death,
Tho' not a word He spoke.

My conscience felt and owned the guilt;
It plunged me in despair;
I saw my sins His blood had spilt,
And helped to nail Him there.

A second look He gave, which said
"I freely all forgive;
This blood is for thy ransom paid:
I die that thou mayst live."

I do believe, I now believe
That Jesus died for me;
And thro' His blood, His precious blood,
I shall from sin be free.

—*John Newton*

1
The Universal Condemnation

As it is written, There is none righteous, no, not one:

There is none that understandeth, there is none that seeketh after God.

They are all gone out of the way, they are together become unprofitable: there is none that doeth good, no, not one (Rom. 3:10–12).

In the first chapter of the book of Romans Paul took a text, just as the apocalypse follows a text. The text is Revelation 1:7, "Behold, he cometh with clouds; and every eye shall see him." The whole twenty-two chapters of the apocalypse are but an unfolding of the text "Christ cometh again."

The text of Romans is the sixteenth verse of the first chapter, our text of this message. Having avowed the theme of his message, Paul proceeded to expound on it.

Fallen Human Nature

The first chapter of the book of Romans describes our fallen human nature. The language is such that the passage is seldom read in public. Yet, as one reads the verses, he will think that the author has visited America and is describing the modern, depraved life of our nation. Iniquity, sin, transgression, shortcoming, and depravity of such degree that they are unthinkable and unimaginable are the beginning of the book of Romans.

In the second chapter of Romans Paul talked about

us, for we have just read the first chapter of Romans. "Therefore thou art inexcusable, O man, whosoever thou art that judgest: for wherein thou judgest another, thou condemnest thyself; for thou that judgest doest the same things" (Rom. 2:1). As we read the first chapter of Romans our response is: "Why, I never did that. He does it, she does it, and they do it over there, those verses describe them, but they do not describe me!" So Paul began the second chapter with our response to this description of fallen human nature, "I am not guilty."

Then he avowed that when one condemns other people, he condemns himself because he does the same things. "Why, that is not so. I never killed anybody. I never murdered anybody." Matthew 5:21–22 says that anger is murder. Were you ever angry? "But I never committed adultery." Matthew 5:28 says that he who looks with desire is an adulterer. "But I never bowed in heathen, pagan worship before images and idols." Colossians 3:5 says that covetousness is idolatry.

Sin is not so much an overt act as it is a state of being. All of us are fallen human beings, and the overt act is but an affirmation and a confirmation of that fallen nature. Paul said that we are guilty of the same sins of those whom we condemn. For example, people who censor are guilty of the same spirit they condemn.

When I was the pastor of a small church in my early ministry, one of the leading deacons came to me and said: "I saw So-and-so drinking beer in a public place. At the next church conference on Saturday afternoon, you must have him come before the church and confess his transgressions and apologize to the church. Else we are going to turn him out, to withdraw fellowship from him; so you arrange for him to be at the conference."

I was just beginning my ministry, and I did not know

many things that I have learned since. So I went to that man and said, "You have been seen by Such-and-such Deacon drinking beer in a public place, and at the next church conference on Saturday afternoon you must come and confess your transgression and ask forgiveness of the church. If you do not we are going to turn you out, to withdraw fellowship from you."

So the man came before the church conference on Saturday afternoon. I stood there before the people and preferred charges against him. He stood up, confessed his transgression, and asked to be forgiven. But as I began to know the deacon who had me do that, the first thing I found out about him was that he sold his corn to a distillery because he could make a little more money that way than selling it to a mill. The second thing I learned as time went on was that he actively campaigned for the repeal of the Eighteenth Amendment, the prohibition amendment. As time continued I found out that he fostered a running feud in the church, dividing it all the time. He was a mean old man; yet he had me hail Bennie before the church because he was seen publicly drinking beer. I had a thousand times rather be the pastor of Bennie who drank beer than of that vicious old deacon who kept the church in a turmoil all the days of his life.

In the little church where I grew up as a boy, there was an aisle down the middle of the church. When we had the Lord's Supper the pastor, in presenting the memorial, said, "All of you who are worthy, sit on the left side of the aisle. All of the rest of you sit on the right side of the aisle." Then they served the elements of the Lord's Supper just to those on the left side of the aisle. I was just a little boy, but I remember looking at all of the worthy ones on the left side of the aisle. Then I looked at all of the unworthy ones on the right side of the aisle. And I tell you truly, it seemed to me that the unworthy ones were better than the crowd on the other side of the aisle.

When I read the story of the prodigal son, I cannot help being impressed with a universal human reaction of the story. The prodigal son wasted his substance with harlots, in drunkenness, and in riotous debauchery. When he came back home to his father's house, the elder brother said: "Father, never at any time have I transgressed thy commandments. I have done everything you asked me to do and have been here all the time, but this, thy son (not my brother) has wasted his substance with harlots and in riotous living." Thereupon, the elder brother refused to go in or to welcome the boy home. He was judgmental; he was censorious; he was critical; he was envious; and he was jealous. As one reads the story, somehow his heart goes out to the repentant prodigal who has turned from his harlots, his drunkenness, and his riotous living. At the same time one's soul recoils from the censorious, critical, hypocritical, and judgmental response of the elder brother. In some ways the elder brother was more of a prodigal than his younger brother.

"Therefore thou art inexcusable, O man, whosoever thou are that judgest: for wherein thou judgest another, thou condemnest thyself; for thou that judgest doest the same things" (Rom. 2:1). That is how the book of Romans begins—with fallen human nature. No one of us is able to point his finger at the other of us and say, "That is you, that is you, and that is you; but I am removed, separate, and apart." All of us are in the same condition.

Finally, Paul concluded the discussion in the third chapter with these famous and oft-quoted words: "There is none righteous, no, not one: For all have sinned, and come short of the glory of God" (Rom. 3:10,23).

Human Attempts Toward Salvation and Justification

Having presented human nature and having presented us, Paul continued in the fourth chapter of Romans with something else that is typical of all of us. It is the natural, carnal response of human nature when we find that we are sinners, when we become aware that we have sinned. There comes a time in every life when we wake up to accountability and we feel ourselves transgressors. A child will feel that he is unworthy in time. That is what it is to be morally sensitive, to be made in the image of God. So as time goes on, all of us reach the age when we feel that we are wrong; we are sinners. Our response is universally alike. There is always an attempt to try to make amends to save ourselves by doing "good deeds."

The apostle used two illustrations of men who sought to find peace with God and salvation by good works. His first illustration is Abraham: "What shall we say then that Abraham our father, as pertaining to the flesh, hath found? For if Abraham were justified by works, he hath whereof to glory; but not before God" (Rom. 4:1–2).

Abraham could possibly boast of his goodness before men, but he could not before God because God knew him intimately. In God's sight Abraham, the father of the faithful and the friend of God, was as deep and abysmal a sinner as anybody else in the sacred pages.

Paul used a second illustration of trying to save ourselves by works. The second illustration is of David, the man after God's own heart. David cried before the Lord and said, "For thou desirest not sacrifices, else would I give it, thou delightest not in burnt offering" (Ps. 52:16). What does a man do when he finds himself in sin and transgression? Good works will not atone for or wash away our sins. Micah uttered that truth when he said: "Wherewith shall I come before the Lord, and bow myself before the high God? shall I come before him with burnt offerings, with calves of a year old? Will the Lord be pleased with thousands of rams, or with ten thousands of rivers of oil? shall I give my firstborn for my transgression, the fruit of my body for the sin of my soul?" (Mic. 6:6–7).

What does a man do when he sins? How can a man be saved who has sinned? Not by good works, the apostle said, for even Abraham was not good enough. David, though he was the king, found nothing material that he could offer to God for atonement—money, his crown, the kingdom, a reformed life, or the keeping of the commandments. We could never be good enough; nor could we ever be rich enough to stand before the holy God.

What is God's response to fallen human nature? What is God's response to human sin? Three times in the fifth chapter of Romans Paul used the illustration of Adam. God's response to human sin is one of judgment and death. "Wherefore, as by one man sin entered into the world, and death by sin; . . . For if by one man's offence death reigned by one; . . . For as by one man's disobedience many were made sinners" (Rom. 5:12,17,19).

God's response is seen in Adam. It is one of immediate death and judgment. "In the day that thou eatest thereof thou shalt surely die" (Gen. 2:17). That day the soul, the spirit of Adam, died, for the image of God was broken. And in the day of the Lord (for a thousand years is as a day to the Lord), Adam's body died. Is not it a strange thing of those ancient men who lived so long, not one of them lived beyond that day of the Lord? Adam lived 930 years. Methuselah, the oldest of all men, lived 969 years. "In the day that thou eatest thereof thou shalt surely die." That day Adam died.

The ground was cursed for his sake. It grew thorns and thistles, and great desert places fell upon the globe. Even the animals that God made became carnivorous. They ate one another. In the millennial picture in the eleventh chapter of Isaiah, the lion will eat straw like an ox. God never made animals to be carnivorous. But when Adam fell, not only was the ground cursed; but the animal world became vicious, full of attack, and began devouring each other.

On that day the first mound in the earth was raised. Beneath it was the son of Adam and Eve, Abel, who died in his own blood. I can picture Adam and Eve standing over that first raised mound with their tears falling to the ground. "In the day that thou eatest thereof thou shalt surely die." Even Adam's other son was cursed with the mark of Cain, placed in his forehead. The whole earth was filled with violence and blood.

Paul said that this is God's response to human sin and our fallen nature. It is one of judgment, wrath, and ultimate and final death. But Paul said something else. As sin brings death, judgment, and the wrath of God, something else moves in the heart of the Lord, for God is also a heavenly Father. "As a father pitieth his children, so the Lord pitieth them that fear him, for he knoweth our frame, he remembereth that we are dust" (Ps. 103:13–14).

As the psalmist says in Psalm 130:3, "If thou, Lord, shouldest mark iniquities, O Lord, who shall stand?" In the great day of his wrath, who could abide the presence of the Lord?

"For the wages of sin is death" (Rom. 6:23). "The soul that sinneth, it shall die" (Ezek. 18:4). But God is also our heavenly Father. Moved with mercy and love, God did something in the beginning; God did something through the centuries; and God did something on a hill called Calvary. How does a man save himself? How do sinners ever stand justified in the presence of God? How do we ever have a right to the pearly city, to the heavenly home? How does God save sinners?

When the Lord drove the man out of the Garden of Eden, at the east gate he placed cherubim. Who are the cherubim? Always in the Bible they are symbols of mercy. They are symbols of forgiveness, of grace. Even on the mercy seat of atonement, the cherubim arch their wings until they touch, looking full upon the blood of expiation. They taught the fallen man how to come back to God. When the boy Abel came before the Lord, he brought a firstling of a flock, a lamb, and there poured out its blood in expiation before the Almighty. In keeping with this heavenly teaching, the sacrifices of the tabernacle and of the temple throughout the pages of the old covenant brought the people before the Lord with blood of expiation. Having learned God's plan and way of atonement through these types, Paul said, "When we were yet without strength, in due time [in God's time] Christ died for the ungodly" (Rom. 5:6). All of the sacrifices of all of the centuries have taught us the meaning of the death of Christ, when the Savior should come and offer atoning sacrifice for us. "God commendeth his love toward us, in that, while we were yet sinners, Christ died for us" (Rom. 5:8). "For if, when we were enemies, we were reconciled to God by the death of his Son, much more, being reconciled, we shall be saved by his life" (Rom. 5:10).

Saved by the blood of the Crucified One,
All hail to the Father, all hail to the Son,

All hail to the Spirit, the great Three in One,
Saved by the blood of the Crucified One.

Glory, I'm saved! Glory, I'm saved!
My sins are all pardoned, my guilt is all gone.
Glory, I'm saved! Glory, I'm saved!
I'm saved by the blood of the Crucified One.[1]

Abraham trusted and believed God, and his faith was counted for righteousness. David came before the Lord and said, "Purge me with hyssop, and I shall be clean: wash me, and I shall be whiter than snow" (Ps. 51:7). That is what it is to be a Christian. Lord, I am not able to cover my sins; I am not good enough to merit—nor am I rich enough to buy—forgiveness; but when I look in trust to Jesus, God does something for me in the blood of the Lamb, in the sacrifice of Christ, and in the atoning grace and mercy of Jesus. My sins are washed away, and I am safe in the arms of Jesus forever.

Could my tears forever flow,
Could my zeal no languor know,

These for sin could not atone;
Thou must save, and Thou alone.

In my hand no price I bring,
Simply to Thy cross I cling.[2]

2
The Doctrine of Total Depravity

> And he released unto them him that for sedition and murder was cast into prison, whom they had desired; but he delivered Jesus to their will.
>
> And as they led him away, they laid hold upon one Simon, a Cyrenian, coming out of the country, and on him they laid the cross, that he might bear it after Jesus.
>
> And there followed him a great company of people, and of women, which also bewailed and lamented him.
>
> But Jesus turning unto them said, 'Daughters of Jerusalem, weep not for me, but weep for yourselves, and for your children.
>
> For, behold, the days are coming, in the which they shall say, Blessed are the barren, and the wombs that never bare, and the paps which never gave suck.'
>
> Then shall they begin to say to the mountains, Fall on us; and to the hills, Cover us.
>
> For if they do these things in a green tree, what shall be done in the dry?
>
> And there were also two other, malefactors, led with him to be put to death.
>
> And when they were come to the place, which is called Calvary, there they crucified him, and the malefactors, one on the right hand, and the other on the left (Luke 23:25–33).

When I was a seminary student, my Greek professor said when we were studying this passage of Scripture: "If you are ever inclined to think too much about human nature, just get a good look at the cross. Look at the cross if you would find human nature exhibited, dramatized, and pictured. That sight is the most tragic and sorrowful of all of the sights in human history."

The doctrine of total depravity is an old-time doctrine of which our forefathers spoke often and emphatically. The teaching is not that a man is as vile as he can be, but that sin, our fallen estate, has entered into every part of human life. Sin is found in our mental faculties, in our emotional natures, in our wills, in our work, in our dreams, in our visions, in the imaginations of our hearts, and in our relationships with one another. We sin in body against ourselves and against others. We sin in our minds; we sin in our volitional natures. The doctrine of human depravity is this: Sin has entered all of our faculties, and we are a fallen people.

One will find in the crucifixion of our Lord a dramatic and emphatic illustration of human nature, a fallen and cursed humanity. Look at the Lord as he is crucified.

Jesus was Perfect

First, was there ever a more beautiful character who lived than Jesus? A man without sin, perfect in all of his life, Jesus possessed a flawless character; yet his people paid false witnesses to vilify him, to defame him, and to debauch his name.

Was there ever anyone who was so gracious in his life and so beautiful in his emotions in the expression of all the good that was in him? Simon Peter referred to Jesus in his sermon in the household of Cornelius as one "who went about doing good" (Acts 10:38). The blessed Jesus brought health, happiness, healing, curing, resurrection, forgiveness, mercy, and heaven wherever he was; that is the Lord.

Yet look at him in that day of the cross. He was brought before Pontius Pilate, the Roman procurator, and was accused officially by the nation of being an insurrectionist and a seditionist—leading his people, they said, to revolt against Caesar and the Roman Empire.

Did ever such gracious words fall from the lips of

a mortal soul? His words were like distilled dew; they were beautiful; they were sublime. And the common people heard him gladly. Everybody understood the Lord. He never went off into deep theological discussions that characterize modern theologists. Jesus spoke in plain language—using parables, heavenly stories with earthly meanings—and his words were light, salvation, and encouragement. The Scriptures say that he preached the good news of the gospel.

But look at the Lord that day of the cross. The Pharisees sought to entrap him. They presented questions that if he answered one way, he would find himself in difficulty; if he answered another way, he would likewise find himself in difficulty. The degradation of humanity!

All of us who have bodies possess some weakness. No one of us has a perfect body or is perfect in our physical frame. All of us exhibit the fall in the Garden of Eden. Every physician could attest to the fact that however strong a man might be, there is always that imperfection. But Jesus had a perfect body, which was formed by the Holy Spirit in the womb of the virgin Mary. I do not know how the Lord looked. Each of us has a mental image of Jesus, and we all think of him as being majestic. There are many little turns in the Scripture story of the Lord that give one that impression.

For example, when the angry crowd sought to take the Lord on several occasions, he just walked through their midst. There was a majesty in the Lord that was magnificent.

But look at him that day of the cross. The Roman soldiers drove great nails through his hands and feet. The fifty-second chapter of Isaiah says that "His visage was so marred more than any man" (v. 14), until he did not look like a man. They beat him; they scourged him; they buffeted him; they plucked out his beard; they spat upon him; and, last of all, as though to thus mar the workmanship of God, a Roman soldier took a spear and opened his side. That is a picture of total human depravity.

Our fallen nature is not something that we just wake up to realize in the day of the cross. Let us look throughout the Bible to see how inexorably and inevitably mankind always falls into the horrible estate of sin and damnation.

Depravity in the Old Testament

First, let us look in the Garden of Eden. God's beautiful creation, the earth, was cursed for our sakes. When sin entered it through Adam and Eve, we fell. "In the day that thou eatest thereof thou shalt surely die" (Gen. 2:17, author's paraphrase). Satan said, "Did God say thou shalt surely die?" That is the first lie. "Ye shall not surely die" (Gen. 3:4). Satan always blinds us and beguiles us. He ruins us and destroys us. He takes away God's word from us. For our sakes, because of our sin, the earth was cursed and has been cursed ever since.

As the days passed God honored his promise, "I will give you dominion over the earth, and all of these things that I have created are under your surveillance, they are in your hands and in your direction" (author's paraphrase). So God made it possible for vineyards to grow. The first thing we read after reading that God destroyed the earth because of its villainy, its iniquity, and its wickedness is that after righteous Noah came out of the ark, he took the beautiful fruit in the vineyards and became drunk.

God gave us language. Animals may have signs and sounds, but a man is the only creation with a language. God gave us language to speak that we might communicate with one another, that we might have poetry, song, and a thousand other things that come from language. Yet at the Tower of Babel the people were blaspheming God and seeking by the genius that God had given them to build them a tower in defiance of Almighty God. The whole earth that the Lord has placed beneath our feet is full of chemicals, minerals, and marvelous, abounding riches; but what does man do with it? He forges explosive bombs and atomic fission out of it to be used for the destruction of cities, and he takes the marvelous principles of science and turns them in such a way that we live in constant fear of one another. The depravity of mankind!

The Lord chose a people through whom he would teach the whole world the oracles of God. He told them, "I have chosen you to be a kingdom of priests, to be the pastors, to be the teachers of all of the families of the earth, that the families of the earth through you may be blessed" (author's paraphrase). The first thing we read is that they fell into grievous sin and error. Ten of them sold their younger brother to be a slave in Egypt. While God was giving them the Ten Commandments, they made themselves naked according to the sexual perversions of the pagans in those days; and they were dancing around and worshiping a golden calf. The story is full of blood and violence.

Depravity in the New Testament

Then finally we come to the New Testament. What a beautiful introduction is presented in the Gospel of Luke! There is the Magnificat of the virgin Mary; there is the responsive song of Elisabeth, her kinswoman; and there is Zacharias who was dumb because he did not believe the angel Gabriel's good news that a son was going to be born to him. Then there is the magnificent praise of Zacharias when the child was born and his lips were unloosed. There is the story of Bethlehem, the angels, the shepherds, and the Wise Men. Truly, it is the most beautiful Christmas story that one could imagine. Yet in the middle of it was bloody Herod with his sword outstretched over Bethlehem, slaying all of the children under two years of age. "In Rama was there a voice heard, lamentation, and weeping, and great mourning, Rachel weeping for her children, and would not be comforted, because they are not" (Matt. 2:18).

Christ set in the earth his church, which he blessed. "Christ also loved the church and gave himself for it" (Eph. 5:25). How sad it is to know the truth of the parables and their true interpretation. Christendom will be like a tree, Jesus said, which grows and grows and finally is filled with every unclean bird. Or, he said, the church is like leaven; and it grows and grows until all of it is leavened. There is corruption in every part of it. There was a time in human history when the church was the dominant political, economic, and social power in the earth; and that period is called the Dark Ages.

We look at our modern day. There has never been any nation as affluent as America. The poorest family living in America today who has a bathroom in the house, water, lights, and a telephone is comparable economically to a family living two hundred years ago who had thirty-one servants. The affluence of America is astonishing; it is overwhelming; it is unlike anything in human history. But has our wealth brought us goodness and virtue?

In a national magazine I saw one of the most penetrating cartoons that I have ever seen. There is a picture of a judge on the bench. Just beyond, in the background, is an arresting officer; and before the bar are three juveniles. The judge is saying to them as he looks down from the bench at the three juveniles: "You belong to the finest families; you live in the most exclusive neighborhoods; you attend the finest schools; and you drive the latest automobiles. No wonder you are juvenile delinquents."

Sociologists and economists say that what we need to solve all of the social unrest in the world today is more, and then they just name *things*—more money, more gadgets, more automobiles, finer houses, finer furniture, finer medical services, finer hospitals, finer everything. My brother, all of the economic policies in the world will not stop depravity. A man is still the same, poor or rich, because it is not money that makes the difference in human character. It is the heart inside. To change the man's clothes does not change the man at all.

A bum will go to a railroad yard, break into a railroad car, and steal a can of tomatoes because he is hungry. Dress him up; send him to college; and he will steal the entire railway system and get away with it. That is the doctrine of total depravity: Sin is in all of our faculties, in all of our lives. One does not escape it in the judiciary or legislative branches of government. One does not escape it in the professional world, in the academic world, or in the ecclesiastical world, the church world. It is everywhere and in you and me. All of us share that fallen nature.

The Lord God sends judgment upon sin which we cannot escape. God said: "The soul that sinneth it shall die" (Ezek. 18:4). "The wages of sin is death" (Rom. 6:23). God himself forged that iron chain, and we cannot break it. Where there is sin, there is judgment; and if that is not true, there is no God. War is a judgment of God upon sinful nations. Stalking crime is a judgment of Almighty God upon our sinful cities. We are afraid to walk the streets of our cities in America.

Drunkenness, alcoholism, is a judgment of Almighty God. In New York City alone there are more than two hundred thousand alcoholics, and there are more than one million family members who are affected by that tragic and abysmal aberration.

Human misery is a judgment of Almighty God upon our sinful lives. One cannot break God's commandments and escape. One might as well jump off the tallest building and say, "Watch me break the law of gravity as I jump off." He simply illustrates the law. It is the same way with God's commandments. One cannot break God's commandments and escape. There is a judgment that is inextricably linked with sin. Since one cannot escape, the personal misery among our people is unbelievable. During every day that passes there are three thousand homes in America that break up. Think of the tears, the heartache, the weeping, the crying, the disappointment, the disillusionment, and the despair that accompany the breakup. God looks down in judgment.

God Gives Us a Way Out

If that were all, Paul would say, "We are of all men most miserable" (1 Cor. 15:19). But God also looks down in mercy, in understanding, in sympathy, in grace, and in forgiveness. God looks down from heaven upon us in our sins and is moved with compassion. That is the gospel; that is the good news that the preacher preaches—that God loves us and sent Jesus to die for us. And to us who will turn, look, accept, believe, trust, and just open our hearts to God, the Lord comes like a flood. He comes with grace, mercy, healing, forgiveness, and salvation. That is the gospel. We are a dying people, yes; we have fallen into sin, yes; all of us have sinned, yes. But the good news is that Jesus died for our sins, that God in love and mercy looked down upon our lost estate and sent his Son to save us. And what a Savior!

Would you like to be happy in your soul, victorious in your life, unafraid to die, unafraid to live? Come, come to Jesus. Whosoever will may come!

3

What It Means to Be Lost

> And it came to pass, . . . that the rich man also died, and was buried;
>
> And in hell he lift up his eyes, being in torments, and seeth Abraham afar off, and Lazarus in his bosom.
>
> And he cried and said, "Father Abraham, have mercy on me, and send Lazarus, that he may dip his finger in water, and cool my tongue; for I am tormented in this flame" (Luke 16:22–24).

Why would one choose to preach on a subject of being lost? It is a terrible, horrible subject. Why choose to speak on what it means to be lost?

First, I did not invent the message. I am an echo, a voice. I only declare what is written on the sacred page.

Second, so many times it has been said that when there used to be hell in the pulpit there was no hell in the streets and in the homes. But when there is no more hell in the pulpit, one finds it now in the streets and in the homes of the people.

Third, it is a merciful revelation from God that there could be such a judgment waiting for those outside of the grace of our Lord. A merciful disclosure does God bring that there is such a place awaiting those who are lost. The same kind of care and concern is shown when a railroad company places a flashing sign across the tracks. It does so not because the company dislikes or hates the people who drive across the roadway, but in mercy. There is danger and the red light flashes because a train is approaching rapidly. So it is with God.

It has been said that there are 240 times in the New Testament where God speaks of hell and damnation. That would be the same thing as if a man were going down a highway and there were 240 signs on the road saying, "This road leads to hell." It is a merciful revelation of God that there is such a judgment and such a damnation.

Here in the book of Luke in chapter 15, the Lord speaks of a sheep that is lost. He speaks of a coin that is lost. He speaks of a boy that is lost. In chapter 16 he speaks of a soul that is lost. In the beautiful story of our Lord in chapter 15, the sheep that is lost is found. The coin that is lost is recovered. The son that is lost is saved. But the soul that is lost is lost forever. In hell the lost man lifted up his eyes, in torment.

Somebody has said, "Apply that word 'lost' to anything and it will spell tragedy." Here is a man who has lost his health. He is cut down in the prime of his life, helpless and unable to sustain himself.

Apply that word to the eyes. Here is a man who has lost his sight and he lives thereafter in darkness and gropes for the wall in blindness.

Here is a man who has lost his mind. I never heard of a sadder story in my life than that of a guard in an asylum who took a young wife and placed her in the cell where her husband was confined, then closed the door. After the time for visiting had expired, he opened the door and saw the young wife kneeling before her husband and crying piteously: "Husband, don't you know me? I am your wife." No recognition came into his face at all. He had lost his mind.

Apply that word *lost* to the soul; and of all tragedies, that is the saddest. There was a most affluent family whose prodigal and wayward son was killed, while drunk, in an automobile accident. They sent for me and said: "The service will be here in the house. Do not read a Scripture. Do not sing a song. Do not read an obituary. Do not call his name. Just say a prayer and we will bury him away."

A Christian can lose his money and the rest of his life live in need, in poverty, and in want. In heaven, all the treasures of God are his. A lost man can live his life in affluence as Dives did. Then he is cut down like a tree. In hell he will lift up his eyes in torment. What good is it to be rich and spend eternity in damnation?

A Christian loses his health; and on the rack of pain, affliction, and agony he spends the rest of his life. In heaven there are no more sick, blind, or crippled. But here is a lost man who lives his entire life in strength and health and then dies. But what is strength and health in damnation and in torment? The grave is the end of all affliction, hurt, trial, and suffering to the Christian. The grave is just the beginning of the torment, affliction, and agony of the lost man who dies.

A liberal theologian said, "If the doctrine of damnation and hell were written on all the pages of all the Bibles of all the world, I would not believe it." Beautifully said, eloquently expressed. That is a fine sentiment, for who could rejoice in the damnation of the lost? But we can hardly dismiss the whole word and revelation of God with that one unbelieving sentence. Contrariwise, the harshest truth that I know in human life and in human history is this: Men are lost without God.

The Sinner Is Lost in This Life

A man without God is lost now. He is lost here. He has no God to whom to pray. He has no Savior with whom to share the burden of his heart and life. He is out of tune with God's universe. The Lord made us for himself, and we are restless and miserable until we rest in him. There is no man happy and at peace outside of the will of God and the call of Christ.

That is the reason that people drink too much. They have to drink to drown themselves from the misery and reality in which they live. As one drunkard said, "It is the shortest way out of Birmingham." Damnation is not just at the judgment bar. Damnation is not just in the eternity to come. Damnation is not just in the fires and torments of hell. Damnation is here. It is in a man's life outside of Christ. It is in a man's soul outside of the will of God. The lost man is lost here in this life.

The Sinner Is Lost in Death

A lost man is lost in the hour of death. To him the grave is an impenetrable darkness, a despair. One time I went through the largest cave in the world, Mammoth Cave in Kentucky. The labyrinth of the vast expanse of that cave is still unmapped after hundreds of years of discovery. In the cave I looked upon the form of a little girl about twelve years of age. The dry atmosphere and the constant temperature of the cave had dehydrated her body. She was a little mummy. She had been lost in the midnight darkness of that endless cavern and finally lay down to die. There she lay, still in the position in which she died, lying on her side, sort of bent over, and with her face in her hands.

As I looked at the child, I could not but think of the horror and the terror of the little girl as she sought light and some way out of the vast darkness that enclosed her. When a lost man dies, that is the way he dies. He faces the midnight of an impenetrable darkness.

A Sinner Is Lost at the Judgment

A lost man is also lost at the great judgment bar of Almighty God. Some day all of us shall stand before God. If there is any one truth revealed in this Holy Book, that truth is this: Someday every soul shall stand in the presence of Almighty God. When the lost man shall stand in the presence of the great judge of all the earth, the Lord God will turn to the recording angel and say, "Do you find his name in the book of life?" The recording angel will turn the pages of the book of life, then will report back to the great Judge, "I cannot find his name." The lost man cries: "O God, you do not understand. Let me explain." The Lord will say: "You have all eternity in which to explain. The judge of all the earth will do right. Speak."

The lost man will say: "O God, you do not understand. I was so busy making money and I was so busy trying to have a good time that I never had time for God. Lord, you do not understand." The Lord will say: "But did I not write in my book, 'It is appointed unto men once to die, but after this the judgment' (Heb. 9:27)? Does a man think, however busy he is making money or having a good time, that he will escape inevitable death?"

He will say: "But Lord, you do not understand. Let me explain. Look at my good works. It has not all been bad, Lord. Look at the good I have done." The Lord will say, "But have I not written in my Holy Word, 'All of our righteousnesses are as filthy rags' (Isa. 64:6)?"

The man will say: "But Lord, you do not understand. Look at all of the churches and denominations down there. I did not know which way to turn. Look at those hypocrites in the church." The Lord will say: "Hypocrites? There are some in my church I know, but nothing like the number out there where you are. Did I say anything about hypocrites? Did I say anything about denominations? Did I not say, 'Believe on the Lord Jesus Christ, and thou shalt be saved' (Acts 16:31)?"

The man will say: "But Lord, you do not understand. Lord, I was waiting for a great feeling. I was waiting for a great experience to pick me up and to set me into the kingdom. I never had a great feeling and a great experience." The Lord says: "Did I say anything about a great feeling? Did I not say, 'Whosoever therefore shall confess me before men, will I confess also before my Father which is in heaven. But whosoever shall deny me before men, will I also deny before my Father which is in heaven' (Matt. 10:32–33)?"

He will say: "But Lord, you do not understand. Lord, I did not intend to be lost. It was never my plan or program in my life that I would be lost. Lord, there just was never a time for me to make a confession of faith in you. I never planned to be lost. I always intended to be saved. It was just some other day and some other time." The Lord will reply: "Did I not write in my book, 'Behold, now is the accepted time; behold, now is the day of salvation' (2 Cor. 6:2)?"

The recording angel will write by the side of his name in the book of damnation: "LOST." The unforgiven sinner is lost. He is lost at the great judgment bar of Almighty God.

The unsaved sinner is lost for eternity. There is no syllable in the book ever of a second chance. As the Bible says, "Where the tree falleth, there it shall be" (Eccl. 11:3). When a man dies without Christ, he dies forever without the Lord. There is no second chance in eternity. He is lost forever. How long is that? Our minds cannot enter into the possibilities.

One time I read that if the world were one vast

circle of solid granite, and a little bird came here to sharpen his beak once every thousand years, when the whole earth had been worn away, one second of eternity will have passed. Our minds cannot enter into God's endless eternity. Lost forever and ever and ever, no opportunity again, no second chance. Dying lost without Christ, without hope, without God. O Lord, how tragic!

One night when I was a boy I awakened in the middle of the night. I was crying as a little boy only could cry. I went to my mother. She said, "Son, why are you crying so?" I replied: "Mother, I dreamed tonight that I was standing at the judgment bar of Almighty God and I was lost. Mother, I was lost!" The terror of that lostness filled my young heart. She talked to me as a mother would to a little boy about Jesus, about the Lord, about the hope that we have in him, that we need never be afraid in him.

When time came for revival, the preacher stayed in our home. Every night after the service he would talk to me about the Lord. In that meeting I was saved. I gave my heart to Christ. I have had the peace that passeth all understanding ever since. That is why when these little children are brought to me, the first question I ask them is this: "If Jesus is the Savior, he necessarily must save us from something. What is it that is so tragic in human life as to bring the Son of God down to earth to die for us?" The answer is because we are lost in our sins. He is a Savior because he saves us from our sins.

Bless his name! Praise his name! Glorify his name! The Son of Man came to seek and to save that which was lost.

4
The Unpardonable Sin

> Wherefore I say unto you, All manner of sin and blasphemy shall be forgiven unto men: but the blasphemy against the Holy Ghost shall not be forgiven unto men.
>
> And whosoever speaketh a word against the Son of man, it shall be forgiven him: but whosoever speaketh against the Holy Ghost, it shall not be forgiven him, neither in this world, neither in the world to come (Matt. 12:31–32).

The possibility that a man could never be forgiven, neither in this world nor in the world to come, is terrifying and horrifying to the soul.

Through the years and the ages people have asked if they could have committed the unpardonable sin, always naming a sin of the flesh. Rarely will one name a sin of the spirit; yet it is the sins of the spirit that are always the more violent and unforgivable.

If one should murder someone in anger, is that the unpardonable sin? Murder could not be the unpardonable sin. Moses in anger struck an Egyptian, murdered him, and hid his body in the sand.

Could it be the lustful sin of adultery, a sin that, more than any other, dissociates the human spirit from God? Could it be the sin of infidelity? No one who ever picked up the Bible is unfamiliar with the sin of David and Bathsheba.

Could it be the sin of denial? Simon Peter cursed and denied that he ever saw or knew the Lord.

Could it be the sin of violence against the church, persecuting, casting it down, blaspheming it? Saul of Tarsus, breathing out threats and slaughter against the disciples of the Lord, persecuted the church even unto strange cities.

One can name every lustful, violent, and angry sin of the flesh. All are forgivable in the sight of God. Then what could be this sin against the Holy Spirit that the Savior says can never be forgiven, neither in this life nor in the life that is to come?

There is only one that I know, and that is the sin against the witness and testimony of the Spirit of God to the saving grace of his Son. Jesus our Lord was conceived, brought into the world, shaped, and formed by the Holy Spirit. His life was dedicated to, filled, and controlled by the Holy Spirit. He was raised from the dead, *horizo,* "pointed out" as the Son of God and the Savior of the world by the Holy Spirit (Rom. 1:4). He is witnessed to in this dispensation and age of grace by the Holy Spirit.

For a man to deny and reject that witness, to call the Holy Spirit in his testimony a liar, is the sin that God will never forgive. The confirmation of that truth in my own study of the Holy Scriptures is this: As deeply as my mind can seek and understand the Bible, the only sin I know at the judgment bar of Almighty God that will condemn a man to everlasting perdition and damnation is that he refused and finally rejected the invitation of the Spirit to trust in Jesus as Savior.

Americans pride themselves upon their realism. They love to say: "Tell it to us straight, Preacher. Do not beat around the bush. Put all the cards on the table. I can take it. Tell us the facts." Let us all be realists and look at the facts honestly, fearlessly. We will choose three facts.

We Shall Not Live Forever

We shall certainly and inexorably die; we will not live forever. "It is appointed unto men once to die, and after this the judgment" (Heb. 9:27). Every cemetery, every grave, and every tombstone is a sermon and a funeral oration about our certain death. Look at that coffin. If one pleases he can choose his coffin now. It will save somebody trouble later on. Man shall certainly die.

God sends his messengers of death before him: the graying of the hair, the crow's feet around our eyes. God sends the lines in our faces and a thousand other messengers into our lives which are knockings at the door. The pale enemy of death is just behind.

In a story of Oriental lore there was a favorite servant who came to his master in Basra and said: "O master, I saw Death on the streets in Basra today. He looked at me. Master, lend me your fleetest horse that I might escape to Baghdad." The master lent him his swiftest horse, and the faithful servant fled to Baghdad. The next day the master, walking down the street of Basra, met Death on the street and walked up to him and said, "Death, what do you mean by frightening my servant so?" Death replied: "Sir, I did not mean to frighten him. I was merely surprised to see him on the street here in Basra because tomorrow I have a date to meet him in Baghdad!" It is appointed unto men once to die. At that exact time, at that exact moment, in that exact place you will certainly die.

We Have No Second Chance

Not in all of the Word of God or in any relevation of the Lord to the human heart has it ever even been suggested that we have a second chance in the grave beyond the day of our death. Ecclesiastes 11:3 reads: "As the tree falleth, there it shall lie." A man's character always tends toward fixation. What a man is, tomorrow he will be more like that. The next day he will be more like it still. As the years pass, he becomes increasingly like that. All character tends toward solidification. God allowed life and character to be so. All of our eternity is just an extension of what we are and know and were in this life. It is remarkable how people are a certain way, a certain kind, perform a certain mannerism, with a certain speech, characterized by a certain gesture.

When I went to Muskogee, Oklahoma, to be pastor of a church, one of the deacons said to me: "On the edge of town there is a man who belongs to our church. He has been stricken and is paralyzed. He is in bed with a stroke. It would be so gracious of you if you would go visit him." I said, "I would be happy to do so."

When I knocked at the door, his dear wife met me at the door. I said: "I am the new pastor of the church and have been told that your husband is ill with a stroke. I have come to see him." She said: "He is in the bedroom. It is such a joy to have you come to see him." She ushered me into the bedroom. I stood and looked at the man on the bed. I said: "I am the new pastor. I heard that you have had a stroke and that you were in bed. I have come to see you." He said, "Gol dang!" I said, "I am just so sorry that you are ill and that you have had the stroke and cannot get out of bed." He said, "Gol dang!" I said: "It is beautiful outside. The sun is shining and everything is so bright. I wish you were out where you could share it." He said, "Gol dang!" I tried something else and after everything I said he would say, "Gol dang!"

After I visited with him, I was so frustrated that I did not know what to think or do. I stood up and was going to ask his wife if I could pray, but he thought I was going to leave. When I stood up he took his hand the best he could and pointed up and said, "Gol dang, gol dang, gol dang, gol dang!" His wife said to me,

"Pastor, he wants you to pray." I said, "Oh, I would be glad to pray." I knelt down by the bed and started praying, "O God in heaven, be good to this man who is so stricken." He said, "Gol dang!" I said, "Lord, in your kindness and goodness raise him up." He said, "Gol dang!" As I prayed my best for him by the side of his bed, after every petition he would say, "Gol dang!" When finally I came to the end of my prayer I said, "Amen." He said, "Gol dang!"

I stood up and said, "God bless you, my brother, until I see you again." He said, "Gol dang!" When I got to the door, turned around for one last word, and said, "Good-bye, my friend," he said, "Gol dang!"

When I got to town I made my way to the deacon who had asked me to visit the stricken man and said to him: "I did what you asked me to do. I went out to visit the man who is ill, and he just says one word." The deacon said to me: "Oh, I forgot to tell you. He had a habit of saying a slang word. He said that slang word over and over all of his life. When he was stricken with his stroke, all of his language left him except that one word." I said: "You do not have to tell me what it is. It is 'Gol dang.' " One of the truest characterizations of human life that I know is this: What you are and what you do finally becomes you. It crystallizes in your character, in your soul.

You might say to a man, "Would you take Jesus as your Savior?" He would say, "No." You would say, "Would you accept the Lord into your heart?" He would say, "No." You would say, "Would you come to church?" He would say, "No." You would say, "Would you pray that Jesus will forgive your sins?" He would say, "No." You would say, "Will you ask God to save you?" He would say, "No." Finally his life will become a negation itself—no, no, no. He will come to the place in his life where he will say it automatically. He will not even think, he will not even be crushed in his heart that he treated Jesus so terribly. He becomes the thing itself. That is human life.

Our Hearts Harden

If the soul did not paralyze, if the heart did not harden, a man could choose the day and hour that he is saved. As the days pass, our wills and our souls and our hearts harden.

My eyes are good; but if I were to cover one of my eyes and leave it covered just for a while, when I took the cover away I could not see out of it. I would be blind in that eye because the nerves would have atrophied.

My ears are good; but if I were to stop one of my ears and leave it stopped for a length of time, I could unstop it, but I could not hear. The nerves and the mechanism would have atrophied.

My arms are well; but one could bind one of my arms to my side and leave it bound there for a certain while and then take the cords away. I could not raise my arm because the muscles and the nerves would have atrophied.

It is the same way with a man's will, heart, and life. When he refuses to respond, the will and heart atrophy. They are paralyzed. They cannot respond. This is not unusual. I sat by the side of a dying old man and did my utmost to win him to Christ. He said, "Somehow I cannot believe." However I prayed, pled, explained, expounded, and made appeal, he died saying those words to me: "Somehow I cannot believe." The soul has its favorable moments, and God has his accepted time. When God says, "Now," and a man says, "No," he is gambling with his soul.

Look at the Bible. The Bible says that when God placed Noah and his family in the ark, God shut the door of the ark. The people to whom Noah had preached had sinned away their day of grace. They had committed the unpardonable sin. For 120 years Noah had preached, preached, and preached. They scoffed, laughed, and ridiculed; then God shut the door. The day of grace had passed.

Lest one think that this theme is just in the Old Testament, it was our Lord himself who said that of the ten virgins waiting for the bridegroom to come, only five entered in. The five foolish virgins who were left out came to the door and said, "Lord, open to us." The Lord answered, "The door is shut." The time had passed. The day of grace was gone.

Esau, for one morsel of meat, sold his birthright. He found no place for repentance, though he sought it carefully with tears. He was rejected of God. In Hebrews we read: "For if we sin wilfully after that we have received the knowledge of the truth, there remaineth no more sacrifice for sins. But a certain fearful looking for of judgment and fiery indignation, which shall devour the adversaries. He that despised Moses' law died without mercy under two or three witnesses: Of how much sorer punishment, suppose ye, shall he be thought worthy, who hath trodden under foot the Son of God, . . . and hath done despite to the Spirit of grace? For we know him that saith, Vengeance belongeth to me, I will recompense, saith the Lord . . . It is a fearful thing to fall into the hands of the living God. For our God is a consuming fire" (Heb. 10:26–31; 12:29).

My father believed in the unpardonable sin. I grew up in a little town where we knew people intimately; my father would say to me: "Son, see that man? He will never be saved." He described to me a time in a revival when we had great outpourings of the Spirit of God. My father would say to me: "I saw that man tremble and weep. I saw the people gather round praying. He stubbornly refused. Son, he will never tremble again. He will never cry again. He will never be under conviction again. He is lost."

Because I was a boy and outlived those people, I eventually saw that my father never failed in his judgment. Every man about whom my father said to me, "He is lost," died lost. As I turn that over in my mind in the years since my father has gone, if my father was sensitive to that, think how much more is God Almighty. It is no wonder the Bible says, "The fear of the Lord is the beginning of wisdom" (Ps. 111:10). Wisdom begins in the awesome reverence of the great God in whose hands the whole world is as dust. The Lord could take our breath away in a moment, could appoint us to die right now, could see that we never rose in life tomorrow. How completely is our destiny in his hands!

What does a man need who says no to Jesus? He needs another sermon? No. He needs another explanation? No. He needs another appeal? No. What does he need? He needs one thing: to move, to respond, to answer. He will never be saved without it.

One could say: "Preacher, I am waiting for a great experience. I am waiting for a great feeling. I am waiting for a marvelous service. I am waiting for that final hour." These are the things by which Satan damns our lives. He will say, "Tomorrow. Not today." What we need is to answer. We need to move, to reply.

In the town in which I went to the seminary, an apartment building about four or five stories high caught on fire one day. The firemen who rushed with all of their equipment to the burning building thought they had everybody evacuated. As they were struggling against the furious flames, to the horror of everybody watching the building burn, a woman appeared at a window on the top floor. In terror and agony she cried for help. The firemen took a life net and gathered around. Pulling it taut, they called up to her and said, "Jump! Jump!" She never leaped. Somehow the fear of jumping into space and into the net on the ground was more than her heart could respond to. She burned to death in the top floor of the apartment building.

Man does not need another explanation, another invitation, another appeal, or another sermon. He needs to move, to respond, to act.

As we have said a thousand times in the appeal, that first step leads us to God. Nailed to the cross, all that dying thief could do was turn his head; but he turned his head and said, "Lord, remember me" (Luke 23:42). God saved him.

One time in a service here in our church a terribly crippled stranger somehow came in the door and sat down at the back of the auditorium. How he got here I do not know. God moved during the service, and the crippled man turned to the people around him on the back rows. He said: "Would somebody help me? I want to go and give my heart to Jesus." There were several in the back who helped that crippled man down the aisle to Jesus. Right there he gave his heart to the Lord.

If all I could do would be to raise my hand in token, God help me to raise my hand. If all I could do would be to blink my eyes, God help me to blink my eyes in token that I open my heart to Jesus. If all I could do is to walk down the aisle, God give me strength to walk down the aisle. It is in acceptance of him that we are saved. There is no other way.

5
The Brazen Serpent

> And Moses made a serpent of brass, and put it upon a pole, and it came to pass, that if a serpent had bitten any man, when he beheld the serpent of brass, he lived (Num. 21:9).

The text of our message today is a type to which our Lord referred in John 3:14–15. Speaking to Nicodemus, the learned ruler and Pharisee and member of the Sanhedrin (the high court of all Jewry), the Lord cited this incident in the twenty-first chapter of Numbers. The story reads: And they [the children of Israel] journeyed from mount Hor by the way of the Red sea, to encompass the land of Edom: and the soul of the people was much discouraged because of the way.

And the people spake against God, and against Moses, 'Wherefore have ye brought us up out of Egypt to die in the wilderness? for there is no bread, neither is there any water; and our soul loatheth this light bread' " (Num. 21:4–5).

Could you find in all of God's Word or in all human experience a sadder commentary on human nature than that? There is a perverseness in us; there is a depth of depravity in us that is almost unfathomable and indescribable. God's gracious care for his people was beautifully exhibited in giving them manna from heaven to eat. The psalmist called it "angels' food" (Ps. 78:25), but the children of Israel murmured against God and against Moses, saying, "Our soul loathes this manna."

"And the Lord sent fiery serpents among the people,

and they bit the people; and much people of Israel died. Therefore the people came to Moses, and said, 'We have sinned, for we have spoken against the Lord, and against thee; pray unto the Lord, that he take away the serpents from us.' And Moses prayed for the people.

"And the Lord said unto Moses, Make thee a fiery serpent, and set it upon a pole: and it shall come to pass, that every one that is bitten, when he looketh upon it, shall live.

"And Moses made a serpent of brass, and put it upon a pole, and it came to pass, that if a serpent had bitten any man, when he beheld the serpent of brass, he lived" (Num. 21:6–9).

The Lord said to Nicodemus, "And as Moses lifted up the serpent in the wilderness, even so must the Son of man be lifted up: That whosoever believeth in him should not perish" (John 3:14–15). To look and live, to believe and be saved, to wash and be clean, is the gospel itself.

The Son of Man Lifted Up

The Son of man shall certainly be lifted up—high, conspicuous, exalted, ascending, lifted up between the earth and the sky—but lifted up not as though he were seated on the throne in Herod's palace or as though he were exalted on a raised dais in the court of Caesar. In earthly life our Lord was lifted up like a dead serpent, hanging and drooping, limp and lifeless on a pole.

There is nothing more assured in all of God's creation than the exaltation of our Lord. He shall be lifted up—high, high, high. The Scriptures say: "Wherefore God also hath highly exalted him, and given him a name which is above every name: That at the name of Jesus every knee should bow, of things in heaven, and things in earth, and things under the earth"

(Phil. 2:9–10). The Lord is supreme over every element in creation.

"Of things in heaven"—the heavenly hosts shall bow in his presence. "Of things in earth"—every soul that has ever lived shall bow in his presence. "Of things under the earth"—even the nether world shall admit the mightiness and the deity of the Lord God. Nothing is more assured than the exaltation of our Savior. Far above all power and principalities, all things present and all things to come, shall our Lord be king and ruler, raised and lifted up. But that ascension and exaltation will not come through hereditary title, political preferment, or military prowess or conquest.

Nor will the Lord ascend to that exalted place in the flaunting of banners, in the blowing of trumpets, or in the acclamation of the people. He shall be lifted up, but it will be like a serpent hanging dead, limp, and lifeless on a pole. He will be exalted, but it will be through suffering, sorrow, and dying. "As Moses lifted up the serpent in the wilderness, even so must the Son of man be lifted up" (John 3:14).

The Plague—Our Death in Sin

It all began in a plague, in a riot of death; it seemed that those venomous vipers were everywhere. They were universal. If a man went into a house, there they were. When he uncovered his bed, there they were. When he sat down to eat, there they were. When he went out into the way, there they were. When those slender, small, tenuous serpents bit, they stung and burned like fire. When they struck, the place on the skin was so small that it was hardly discernible; but on the inside of the victim's body there was fever, convulsion, and death.

This is a type used by our Lord of the universal depravity of the human heart, the universal presence of sin in human life. This depravity is in our hearts, our houses, our homes, our uprisings and our downsittings, our goings forth and our comings back, our relationships in life. Inexorable and inescapable is the universal presence of sin and of death. Humanity is a depraved and a fallen race; and however we philosophize, rationalize, or extenuate, the harshest fact in human life and in human history is this: Men are lost in sin and transgression. We are dead in our sins. Sin is present universally.

Not only is that true, but these serpents are a type of the destructive and wasting power of sin. How the fiery venom of sin everywhere in the earth wastes and destroys!

The strongest man who ever lived, shorn of his locks, his eyes blinded, and bound hand and foot, ground at the prison mill around and around and around. With the uncircumcised, blaspheming Philistines mocking his God, Samson bowed his head and prayed, "[Lord,] Let me die with the Philistines" (Judg. 16:30). Oh, the wasting, destroying power of sin!

Solomon, the wisest man who ever lived—how auspicious and august was the introduction of his reign. The Lord loved him, and God sanctified and hallowed every word that he said and every kingly deed that he did. But as the years passed, his heart turned away through sin; and he left to his son a dissolving and a divided kingdom.

The man after God's own heart, King David, fell into terrible transgression. God's prophet, Nathan, came before him and said, "And the sword shall never depart from thine house" (2 Sam. 12:10). The history of the house of David is written in blood, in tears, and in death. "The soul that sinneth, it shall die" (Ezek. 18:4); "the wages of sin is death" (Rom. 6:23).

Those venomous, fiery serpents were everywhere.

And the people were dying in physical death, in spiritual death, in moral death, in the second death, and in eternal death.

Also, the type of the brazen serpent portrays our helplessness before death. How inescapable and incapable is humankind before the judgment of death! We have lived on this earth for thousands and thousands of years, but in sin and in death we are the same now as we were then. Mankind has lifted itself out of ignorance, superstition, and a thousand other darknesses; but in our hearts, in our souls, we are still just the same. Our technological achievements are fantastic. What science, knowledge, and understanding have done for the human race in its advancement is almost beyond what whole libraries can describe; but we are still on the same moral, spiritual plane with Adam and Eve. We have never found a way out from the universal affliction, waste, destruction, and judgment of sin. We are a dying people.

The Remedy—the Death of Sin

Moses, hearing the cry of the throng, took the problem to God. I can hear Moses as he spoke to God: "Lord, the people are dying. The serpents are everywhere." And God said to Moses, "Cast a brazen serpent, put it on a pole, and raise it up in the midst of the camp, and it shall be if a man is bitten and dying, if he looks, he shall live" (author's paraphrase).

That is one of the most astonishing things that I find in human experience. If one goes to a hospital and there is a sign on that hospital, it will be a pole with two serpents wrapped around it. If one sees a doctor's car and he has a sign on his car, it will be that same caduceus. If one sees a special stationery which is used by a person in a healing profession, on it will be that caduceus. When one turns the pages of history, there will be that same sign of health and healing. How astonishing that the sign of health, of healing, of deliverance, and of salvation should be a serpent hanging on a pole! Not a real serpent because a venomous snake, killed and draped over that pole, would have only served to remind us of how many others were still alive. It would have been just another snake that should have been killed. Not a real snake—not a real serpent—but a representative serpent, one cast out of brass and raised high on that pole, lifeless, dead, with its fangs extracted, limp, with no more power to sting, to bite, and to kill.

The same is true with the Son of God. "As Moses lifted up the serpent in the wilderness, even so must the Son of man be lifted up" (John 3:14). Like a serpent, dead, hanging on a pole. He is the representative man, not another sinner who should have been there dying for his own transgressions. He is not one of us who deserve to die because of our sins; he is not just another crucified thief hanging there on the tree. Rather, he is the representative man, the God-man Christ Jesus, dying, hanging on a tree. In him was injected all of the poison from the sins of the entire human race. Jesus was made to be sin for us, he who knew no sin, that we might be made the righteousness of God in him. The Lord was made sin for us and died sin-condemned, sin-judged, and sin-helpless. He was so certainly dead that there was no second blow needed; no bone was broken. Our Lord was certainly dead. The great representative man was dying for the sins of the whole world.

The Call to Look and Live

"That whosoever believeth in him should not perish but have eternal life" (John 3:16). To look and live, to believe and be saved, to wash and be clean! Oh, the incomparable and inscrutable ways of the Almighty that we are saved by a look, that we are saved by a trust, that we are saved by the moral act of acceptance! A man who had just been bitten could look; a man who was almost gone could look, just look. It was a moral act. When the man looked he showed that he believed God's Word and promise; he accepted God's healing and God's salvation.

In the type is also a part of that unfathomable mystery that ever characterizes God. There is a mystery in the mercy of God, in the saving power of the cross, into which mind cannot enter. But that is God, and that is God's provision for the saving of the lost. It is God who saves us.

The woman with an issue of blood came into the throng behind our Lord. She reached forth and touched the hem of his garment. How does the hem of a garment save? It does not; but the woman said in her heart, "If I may but touch his garment, I shall be whole" (Matt. 9:21). The healing is in God; it is God who heals.

So it is on the cross. It is the pouring out of the life of our Lord that heals, that saves. A man takes it as a gift. He receives it in the love and mercy of God. The saved man accepts the promise, for "God said it and I trust Him." "Look and live," God said. "Believe and be saved," God said. "Wash and be clean," God said. There is a mystery in our salvation known but to God, and it is a part of the infinitude of the love and provision of the Lord.

The man crucified next to Jesus turned to him on the cross and said, "Lord, remember me when thou comest into thy kingdom" (Luke 24:42); and the Lord said, "Today shalt thou be with me in paradise" (Luke 24:43). Who could say that but the Lord? God does the saving. These who are most dear to us—when the time comes for them to die, all we can do is to bury them out of our sight, to lay them away. Only God can receive us himself; only God can say, "Today shalt thou be with me in paradise." Only God can stand by the side of the bed of death and say to the trusting soul, "Today you are coming to my house; today you are to be with me; today you are to cross the swollen river; today you are to enter into the kingdom; today you will be crowned." We are so helpless as human beings. Only God can save us, and that atoning grace is poured out in a cleansing fountain in the cross to which we look and live.

When Spurgeon was a young man, lost, he wandered out of a storm into a little chapel. The chapel was too small to have a minister, but there was a layman there who was expounding in his stuttering tongue and faltering language the great passage of Isaiah, "Look unto me, and be ye saved, all the ends of the earth: for I am God, and there is none other" (Isa. 45:22). And as he spoke he pointed to young Spurgeon and said: "Young man, you look so miserable. Look to Jesus." Spurgeon said, "That night I looked and I lived."

> I have a message from the Lord, hallelujah!
> It is only that you look and live.
>   Look and live, my brother, live;
>   Look to Jesus Christ and live.
> 'Tis recorded in His word, Hallelujah!
> It is only that you look and live.[1]

The acceptance of what God has done for us, the gratitude for the manna, the thanksgiving for the water of life, the opening of the soul to the God who can do for us what we cannot do for ourselves or for one another, the looking in expectation of the healing from his divine and omnipotent hands—when you do that, just *that,* you are saved. That is what it is to be a Christian, a follower of Christ.

His forever, only his;
Who the Lord and me shall part?
Ah, with what a rest of bliss
Christ can fill the loving heart!

Heav'n and earth may fade and flee,
Firstborn light in gloom decline;
But while God and I shall be,
I am his, and he is mine.[2]

6
The Wounds of Jesus

After this, Jesus knowing that all things were now accomplished, that the scripture might be fulfilled, saith, I thirst.

Now there was set a vessel full of vinegar: and they filled a sponge with vinegar, and put it upon hyssop, and put it to his mouth.

When Jesus therefore had received the vinegar, he said, 'It is finished': and he bowed his head, and gave up the ghost.

The Jews therefore, because it was the preparation, that the bodies should not remain upon the cross on the sabbath day, (for that sabbath day was an high day,) besought Pilate that their legs might be broken, and that they might be taken away.

Then came the soldiers, and brake the legs of the first, and of the other which was crucified with him.

But when they came to Jesus, and saw that he was dead already, they brake not his legs:

But one of the soldiers with a spear pierced his side, and forthwith came there out blood and water.

And he that saw it bare record, and his record is true; and he knoweth that he saith true, that ye might believe (John 19:28–37).

The crucifixion of our Lord is dramatically portrayed in each of the four Gospels. Most of the gospel message is taken up with the story of the suffering of our Lord. His ministry was spread over three years; yet all four of the Gospels spend most of their words in recounting the suffering, the crucifixion, and the ultimate resurrection triumph of our blessed Savior.

Not spiritualizing as such, we are going to look at the body of Jesus in a little different way than just beholding him as he was nailed to the cross. We will take the presentation of the incarnation of our Lord today and what we do today to bruise, wound, and tear the flesh of our Lord. In the days of his actual flesh, the guards drove great nails through his hands and his feet. One of the soldiers took a spear and thrust it into his side. When Jesus died there were five wounds so visible, so red, so crimson—the blood flowing from his two hands, from his two feet, and from his side. It is easy to visualize the awful tragedy of earth's darkest day when the gift that God made in Bethlehem was handed back to God on the point of a Roman spear. I would suppose that the cross was first laid on the ground and the soldiers took the body of Christ and laid him on top of the cross with his back against the wood. Then one of the soldiers must have taken Jesus' right hand and driven a great, heavy nail through it. Following that, another soldier took his left hand and drove a heavy spike through his left hand. Then one of the soldiers took his feet, crossed one on top of the other, and drove one of those long, heavy nails through his feet. While all of that was going on, would you think that he cried, would you think that he lamented? The fifty-third chapter of Isaiah says, "As a sheep before her shearers is dumb, so he openeth not his mouth" (Isa. 53:7).

That was the crucifixion of our Lord. He did not cry. There was no sound in his intense suffering.

The Lord is incarnate in his church. When he met Paul on the way to Damascus, Christ cried to him, "Why persecutest thou me?" Paul said, "Who art thou?" and the Lord said, "I am Jesus whom thou persecutest" (Acts 9:4–5). When Paul was wasting the church, he was wasting the Lord. When he was wounding the church, he was wounding the Lord.

When we identify the Lord today with his people, we are doing nothing other than what the Scriptures present of our Master. Is it possible today to wound

Christ, to drive great stakes through his hands and feet, to thrust a spear into his side?

We Can Wound the Lord by Leading His Children Astray

First, we can wound the Lord today by leading astray his children, especially his little ones. "Then said he unto the disciples, 'It is impossible that offences will come: but woe unto him, through whom they come! 'It were better for him that a millstone were hanged about his neck, and he cast into the sea, than that he should offend one of these little ones' " (Luke 17:1–2).

We wound the body of Christ, we drive nails into his flesh and thrust a spear into his heart, when we place stumbling blocks before his little ones. That can be interpreted in two ways, and I think both ways are correct. His little ones are children, and his little ones are those who have just been saved. They are babes in Christ. When we lead them astray, we wound the body of our Lord.

There are many ways in which we can lead astray our children, our little ones; and I am going to illustrate one. When one sees a drunkard in the gutter sitting in his own vomit, there is not a boy or girl who, looking at the drunkard, would think that the man is a paragon of someone the child would like to be. Rather, the child would be offended by the sight, the scene, the smell, the filth, and the dirt. There is nothing more unbecoming, unpalatable, unseemly, or unsightly than the alcoholic in his stupor, in his drunkenness, and in his vomit. There is no youngster who would not be affected by such an example.

But the child and the young executive are led astray,

are hurt by the example of a fine, successful, but non-Christian, businessman. Naturally, the young fellow would like to be like him; he is a successful doctor, he is a famous lawyer, or he is a businessman of great influence. Just to look at him is to want to emulate him; he is successful. When the youngster sees the successful man drink liquid pot, take a drug—not just heroin, hashish, marijuana, or any other derivative of the poppy plant, but anything that affects a man's mind, including alcohol, is a drug—then he is badly influenced to do likewise. When we work to get our youngsters not to use drugs and the finest people use them all the time, how on earth can one turn to the youngster and say, "Under no condition are you to find yourself a victim of drugs."

The curse of America and the world is a thousand times more widespread in alcohol than it is in heroin or opium of any kind. The curse of the drug problem is the curse of the liquor traffic. When a fine executive drinks, takes liquid pot, the boy watching him sees no reason at all why he should not also emulate him. Look what a fine, acceptable, and successful professional man or businessman he is. That leads the youngster astray. These statistics are not just factual; they are everywhere. Of men who drink, eight of them can get by with it all right, but the ninth one is destroyed; he becomes a problem drinker; and he ruins his life, himself, his home, his job, his effectiveness as a man. A thousand times better is it for the man to say, "I may be able to carry my liquor, I may be able to smoke my drugs without personal harm; but for the sake of those youngsters, those teenagers, and those young executives who are coming along, I will not wound the body of Christ; I will not partake for his sake. I will not drink."

One of the tragedies that overwhelmed American life was the destruction of the Eighteenth Amendment, for America was persuaded that we were on the downbeat in the days of prohibition. If we are honest, there was never a greater period in American history than the days or prohibiton. I quote just one statistic from the best-known criminologist of those days: "Let us take courage from the official record covering the eighteen years 1910 to 1927 inclusive, which shows a marked decline of thirty-five to forty percent in the crime rate in the United States, and this notwithstanding the 'new' crimes resulting from liquor, drug, and traffic laws enacted since 1910."

What is the crime rate doing in America today? It is soaring and increasing in such an upward spiral that we are becoming a nation of fear. We cringe before our city streets. There are great sections of the great metropolitan areas in the United States where even a man hardly walks without fear. Offending these little ones, wounding the body of Christ.

There is admonition against drinking in the Bible. I am saying that when one takes drugs—liquid, white tablet, or marijuana—when one takes drugs of any kind, he is setting an example before a youngster who might see and know, before a young executive who is following along in the drug-taker's footsteps. His imitation may destroy his life. The risk is not worth it; I do not care how much personal joy and pleasure one might think he would derive from it. I have never understood why a man has to have liquor in order to carry on a conversation or to have a good time. How does one fathom that a deep, dark hangover is having a good time? One does not need it. When we walk before God and before these young people, in the fear and love of the Lord, they are blessed; you are blessed; and the body of Christ is not wounded.

Men of the Cloth Can Wound the Lord by Their Attack Upon the Christian Faith

Second, we wound the body of our Lord in the tragedy that we find in so many of our modern pulpits and divinity schools. The apostle Paul said: "And their word will eat as doth a canker: of whom is Hymenaeus and Philetus; Who concerning the truth have erred, saying that the resurrection is past already; and overthrow the faith of some" (Tim. 2:17–18).

For a man in a divinity school or in a church-related school to stand up in his professorial capacity and mock, make fun, and ridicule the Word of God is tragically becoming commonplace. When one sends a boy to a state university and he studies under a professor who is an infidel—who mocks, derides, and scoffs at the Word of God—that has a strong effect upon the youngster because he has not expected that in a Christian school. State universities have infidels who openly teach there; they have agnostics and atheists who teach there. When the agnostic and the atheist stand up at a state university and deride, scorn, mock, and ridicule the Word of God, the boy expects it.

But when one sends a child to a church-related school, which has the name of the denomination which supports it, and a professor mocks and ridicules the Word of God, the boy is destroyed in his very soul! To send a boy to the seminary, to the divinity college, where the professor casts doubt at the validity of the virgin birth, the resurrection of our Christ, his promised return, and our own hope of seeing him in the flesh as Job cried, "Yet in my flesh shall I see God" (Job 19:26), the boy is destroyed, the kingdom of God is hurt, and Jesus is wounded.

An editorial from a Chicago newspaper talking about professors who are scoffing and deriding the Word of

God said: "We are struck with the hypocrisy and the treachery of these attacks on Christianity. This is a free country and a free age and men can say what they choose about religion, but this is not what we arraign these divinity professors for. Is there no place to assail Christianity but a divinity school? Is there no one to write infidel books except professors of Christian theology? Is a theological seminary an appropriate place for a general massacre of Christian doctrine? We are not championing either Christianity or infidelity but only condemning infidels masquerading as men of God and Christian teachers."

A teacher friend of mine attended Chicago University in order to get his Ph.D. degree in pedagogy. While he was there he became acquainted with a young man who was in the Chicago Divinity School. The young fellow was a Presbyterian. So the day came when the young man in the divinity school was graduated and a Presbyterian church in the Midwest called him. He went to my friend and said: "I am in a great quandary; I am in a dilemma. I do not know what to do. I have been called to this church, and it is an old-fashioned Presbyterian church that believes in the Bible. I do not believe the Bible, and I do not know what to do."

My friend said to him, "I can tell you exactly what to do." The young preacher asked, "What?" The friend said, "I think you ought to quit the ministry."

I say the same thing. If a young fellow has come to the place where he does not believe the Word of God and he cannot accept the divine mind of God as it is revealed in the blessed Lord Jesus who was born miraculously, who was raised miraculously, whose whole life was a miracle—if he cannot believe that and preach that, I think he ought to quit the ministry. It wounds the body of Christ for his servants to stand up and reject the marvelous truths that the Lord hath given to us in the holy Scriptures and in the life, ministry, testimony, birth, resurrection, and promised return of our blessed Jesus.

We Can Wound the Lord by Our Indifference

A third way that we can wound the body of our Lord is by sheer indifference. Following the life of the apostle Paul when he came to Athens, we read: "Then certain philosophers of the Epicureans, and of the Stoics, encountered him. And some said, What will this babbler say? other some, He seemeth to be a setter forth of strange gods: because he preached unto them Jesus, and the resurrection" (Acts 17:18). When Paul spoke of the resurrection, some of them laughed out loud. Others more courteously said, "We will hear thee again of this matter" (Acts 17:32) and smilingly walked away. Oh, for anything except just to pass Jesus by!

Lord Hugh Cecil, son of the famous Lord Salisbury, premier of Great Britain, said one time that the great danger that threatens us is not that people will regard Christ as untrue, but that they will come to regard him as unnecessary. The conquests of medical science and social reform are helping lessen belief in sin and, consequently, belief in the need of a divine Savior.

More and more there is developing the attitude that there is nothing pertinent, nothing that a man ought to weep over, nothing that a man ought to consider now in Christ. Men just pass him by.

Anything but just to pass him by, as though his tears were nothing, his wounds were nothing, his cross is nothing, his poured-out life for us is nothing—anything but just to pass him by.

O Lord, how could any heart be so calloused, any soul be so hardened as to look upon our Lord and say: "It matters nothing to me. It has no meaning to me. There is no pertinency for me."

O Master, just to behold, to look, is to be convicted. Just to remember what God did in his Son for us is to praise his name, to love him, to return words of gratitude to him. And that is what it is to be a Christian.

Lord, I do not forget, this you did for me; this, I shall do for thee: dedicate thee my life, give thee my heart in faith and trust, give thee my soul some day in the hour of my dying, and plead the mercies of Christ when I stand at the judgment bar of Almighty God. That is what it is to be a Christian, to accept Jesus, his grace, and his love.

PART 2

The Cross—Our Atonement

And almost all things are by the law purged with blood; and without shedding of blood is no remission.

It was therefore necessary that the patterns of things in the heavens should be purified with these; but the heavenly things themselves with better sacrifices than these.

For Christ is not entered into the holy places made with hands, which are figures of the true; but into heaven itself, now to appear in the presence of God for us:

Nor yet that he should offer himself often, as the high priest entereth into the holy place every year with blood of others;

For then must he often have suffered since the foundation of the world: but now once in the end of the world hath he appeared to put away sin by the sacrifice of himself.

And as it is appointed unto men once to die, but after this the judgment:

So Christ was once offered to bear the sins of many; and unto them that look for him shall he appear the second time without sin unto salvation (Heb. 9:22–28).

There Is a Green Hill Far Away

There is a green hill far away,
Without a city wall,
Where the dear Lord was crucified,
Who died to save us all.

We may not know, we cannot tell
What pains He had to bear;
But we believe it was for us
He hung and suffered there.

He died that we might be forgiven,
He died to make us good,
That we might go at last to heaven,
Saved by His precious blood.

There was no other good enough
To pay the price of sin,
He only could unlock the gate
Of heaven and let us in.

Oh, dearly, dearly has He loved,
And we must love Him, too,
And trust in His redeeming blood,
And try His works to do.

—Cecil F. Alexander

7

How the Death of Christ Saves Us

> And as Moses lifted up the serpent in the wilderness, even so must the Son of man be lifted up:
> That whosoever believeth in him should not perish, but have eternal life (John 3:14–15).

There are many theories of the atonement (how the death of Christ saves us). Throughout the centuries there have been men who have tried to expound the reason for the efficacious offering of the Son of God. There is the patristic explanation, that of the early church fathers and their penal theory. There is the Anselmic theory that the atonement honored God's sense of justice and righteousness. Another theory was the Socinian theory, that the death of Christ was that of an example, a paragon that he died as a martyr dies or a hero dies. There were also the Grotian and the Bushnellian theories.

While I was in the seminary, one of my minors was the atonement. Even after studying the atonement for two years and after I had passed a doctor's examination on the subject, I felt that the mystery of the death of Christ was as unfathomable and as inexplicable as the day that I began the survey.

There is a mystery in the death of Christ that man's mind cannot enter. There is something in God, in the Holy Spirit, and in Christ in the forgiveness of our sins that is a mystery into which only the mind that could equal the mind of God could ever be commensurate. But there are some things that a rational human being, one who can understand and sense, can see. We can see what God is like, what God does, and how God does it—which is all that a human being can see anyway, for no man can explain anything. He merely sees and describes what he sees, but the intricate details that lie back of its being, we do not enter into; we just see the result.

So the marvelous mystery—inexplicable, unfathomable, indescribable—of the atoning grace of God and the death of Christ is beyond what we are able to encompass in theology or in sermon.

There Is Death in Sin

Here is one thing we can see. There is something in God that put these two together—sin and death. God welded the link together in the beginning, and no man has ever been able to unweld the iron chain that steadfastly and eternally holds them. Sin and death: "The wages of sin is death" (Rom. 6:23); "The soul that sinneth it shall die" (Ezek. 18:20); "In the day that thou eatest thereof thou shalt surely die" (Gen. 2:17). When God pronounces judgment upon transgression the result is death. The day one sins, he begins to die.

But the same Lord God who pronounced that judgment upon our sins—physical death, moral death, spiritual death, the second death, eternal death—also did something else. God said that atonement could be vicariously made. Somebody else could die in our stead. Somebody else could suffer in our death. If that vicarious suffering were of a nature as to satisfy God, we who have sinned can go free.

Sometimes the Bible describes that redemption in terms of a ransom. A slave is taken into captivity and is sold. We in sin are like that. As the Scriptures say of us, "[We are] sold under sin" (Rom. 7:14). We are in the bondage of sin. But somebody could pay our debt; somebody could ransom us; somebody could buy us back. That is a presentation in the Scriptures of the grace of Christ. The Scriptures say, "Ye are not your own . . . Ye are bought with a price" (1 Cor. 6:19–20). "For the Son of Man came not to be ministered unto, but to minister, and to give his life a ransom for many" (Mark 10:45). Somebody else can pay our debt and our penalty, and we can go free.

Most of the time our redemptive salvation is presented in the Bible under the figure, the picture, the typology, and the symbolism of one who is shedding blood—that is, pouring out his life for us.

In the days of the Passover God said, "My angel of death will visit the land of Egypt, but it shall be that if there is blood sprinkled on the lintels and on the doorposts, the angel of death will pass over; and there will be life in that home" (author's paraphrase). All that a man had to do to be saved, to be delivered from the judgment that night in Egypt, was to find safety under the blood. God did the necessary action. When the angel saw the blood, he passed over. Vicariously an offering is presented—in this instance, a lamb.

The Day of Atonement presented this same picture of atoning grace. Two sacrificial animals were chosen; one was slain, its blood caught in a basin. The high priest entered into the holy of holies beyond the veil and took the blood and sprinkled it upon the propitiatory, the mercy seat. Then the second sacrificial animal was brought before the high priest, who had come out of the holy place. The high priest laid both of his hands on top of the animal and confessed all the sins of the people. Then the animal (called the "scapegoat," for in its atoning blood human sins were taken away) was taken out to a place far away and driven off. That, like the picture, was in the whole sacrificial system.

Twice every day the lamb was slain and offered as a burnt sacrifice for the sins of the people. Mostly it will be under the figure, which God will teach us, that in the shedding of blood there is remission of sin.

The Lamb of God, Jesus, Pays Our Debt of Sin

If our blood were shed, we could not atone for anyone else because we ourselves are sinners. When we die, we just pay the penalty for our own sins. But all of the sacrificial system of the Old Testament—the Day of Atonement, the Passover feast, and so forth—all of those were pictures and types of him who was the Lamb of God and the Lord in heaven. Our Father so values the priceless life of Jesus that the sacrifice of the Prince of Glory is commensurate with all of the sins of all the world. As in the days of the Passover, if one was under the blood, God gave him life for death.

And so it is with us. God so values and prizes the blood of Jesus that if one trusts in his son, God considers the atoning death of our Lord as more than grace sufficient to wash away all of our sins, "For the wages of sin is death; but the gift of God is eternal life through Jesus Christ" (Rom. 6:23).

In Romans 5:1–10 we read: "Therefore being justified by faith, we have peace with God through our Lord Jesus Christ: By whom also we have access by faith into this grace wherein we stand, and rejoice in hope of the glory of God. And not only so, but we glory in tribulations also: knowing that tribulation worketh patience; And patience, experience; and experience, hope: And hope maketh not ashamed; because the love of God is shed abroad in our hearts by the Holy Ghost which is given unto us. For when we were yet without strength, in due time Christ died for the ungodly. For scarcely for a righteous man will one die: yet peradventure for a good man some would even dare to die. But

God commendeth his love toward us, in that, while we were yet sinners, Christ died for us. Much more then, being now justified by his blood, we shall be saved from wrath through him. For if, when we were enemies, we were reconciled to God by the death of his Son, much more, being reconciled, we shall be saved by his life."

God so values the death of his Son that if anyone will trust in Jesus, God says that trust is equal, all-sufficient for the washing away of all of his sins.

The Holy Spirit has the power to apply that message to the human heart. Let me illustrate that miracle of the Holy Spirit by a comparison. One could study extensively about the martyrs, the heroes, the Nathan Hales who say, "I only regret that I have but one life to lose for my country." We admire and praise God for a patriot like Nathan Hale. The sacrifice of men like him made our nation what it is. The pouring out of blood for freedom, for liberty, and for the protection of our homes and families has been the story of martyrdom, bloodshed, and heroic dedication through the years.

When I speak of the martyr's death and the hero's death, the people who listen say: "What a noble dedication. We ought to appreciate the liberties and freedoms which have come to us through their sacrifices." But in the gratitude and admiration of that sacrifice and dedication, no one is ever convicted of his sins. No one would be drawn to a new life in repentance, in confession, and in faith. But when a man anywhere presents the death, the sobs, the tears, the flowing wounds of Jesus, God's Holy Spirit does something in the hearts of the people. There is a conviction of sin. We cry, "I am not what I ought to be; I am not what I could be; by God's grace I am not what I am going to be." There is a conviction of sin in our hearts. We sense our shortcomings, our derelictions, our failures, and our transgressions. That is the work of the Holy Spirit.

The Holy Spirit does something else. He points to the cross; he points to Jesus; he points to the Lamb of God. And he does it in wooing grace, in loving invitation and appeal. "Look," the Holy Spirit says. That is why any time there is a teaching that emphasizes the Holy Spirit alone, it is a teaching the opposite of what the New Testament doctrine is—for the Lord said, "The Holy Spirit shall not speak of himself; he will not draw attention to himself." The work of the Holy Spirit serves someone else.

The Holy Spirit exalts Jesus, points to Jesus, and brings our hearts to Jesus. When a man speaks about the grace and the love of God in Christ Jesus, something happens to him. We look and look and look; then one day we see. We listen and listen; then one day we hear. The gospel message is pressed to the heart of the person hungry for fulfillment by the power of the Holy Spirit.

Sometimes I see people weep. Why do they cry? Just thinking about the Lord, just looking again, just seeing Jesus. Almost always there will be an experience in the life of a child when the child will cry before the Lord. Why? Just looking at Jesus, the power of the cross of Christ. That is the work of the Holy Spirit. God is so near and so dear that we are overcome. Not only does God count the blood of Christ all-sufficient for our sins; and not only does the Holy Spirit press the message of saving grace to our hearts; but we sense and feel his presence. I have always thought that far more important than an intellectual understanding of the death of Christ is the feeling of his presence in our souls, the realization of him in our deepest hearts. This he did for me.

Saved by the Intercessory Life of Our Lord

God also says, "For if when we were enemies [sinners, recalcitrants, unrepentants, unregenerates], we were reconciled to God by the death of his Son (God says that in Christ our sins are all washed away and that the debt has been paid), much more, being reconciled, we shall be saved by his life" (Rom. 5:9). By "his life" Paul was referring to the Lord's resurrected life. If in the cross of Christ—if in the death of Jesus our sins are all paid, we have been reconciled to God, God is favorable toward us, and he has forgiven us and welcomes us—then we are even more certainly assured of our salvation. I think of that in three ways.

First, he comes to live in our hearts and in our homes. Jesus is here. We can feel and sense his presence. The Lord said: "Behold, I stand at the door and knock: if any man hear my voice, and open the door, I will come in to him and will sup with him, and he with me" (Rev. 3:20). We can have fellowship with God.

> I walk with the King, hallelujah!
> I walk with the King, praise His name!
> No longer I roam, my soul faces home,
> I walk and I talk with the King.[1]

If we have been reconciled by the death of his Son, much more shall we be saved by his life.

Second, not only is Christ with us living in our hearts; but the Scriptures say, "He is able also to save them to the uttermost that come unto God by him seeming he ever liveth to make intercession for them" (Heb. 7:25). He prays for us and intercedes for us. He pulls for us; he helps us. He is in heaven, and our Lord bows down his ear to hear his people when they pray. He reaches down with helping hands of encouragement, sympathy, and understanding.

What a friend we have in Jesus,
All our sins and griefs to bear!
What a privilege to carry
Everything to God in prayer! [2]

Third, in the final hours of my death, who can go with me across that dark and swollen river? Can you? When that hour comes, I will have to face it alone. That is why it is such a tragedy to die lost. Nobody to help, no Savior, no Lord. Just dying alone.

In the closing of *Pilgrim's Progress,* when the time came for Pilgrim to cross the swollen river, the trumpet sounded on the other side and one of God's saints went home. When we die we have a coronation day. It is the greatest day and the sublimest hour of our life, for Christ is with us to receive us to himself. He is on the other side of the river—not here, but there. Our home is there; our inheritance is there; and our Lord is there. We are saved by his life, received into glory, welcomed by his precious hands. As one of our eloquent preachers used to say, "The pierced hands of Jesus who opened for us the doors of grace shall open for us the gates of glory." Oh, what it means to be a Christian, to love the Lord!

8
Bearing Our Sins Away

And almost all things are by the law purged with blood; and without shedding of blood is no remission.

And as it is appointed unto men once to die, but after this the judgment:

So Christ was once offered to bear the sins of many; and unto them that look for him shall he appear the second time without sin unto salvation (Heb. 9:22,27–28).

The world repudiates the gospel of blood redemption and salvation. Men state their refusal bluntly, crudely, rudely, and brutally. They say if we have tractors to move mountains, we do not need faith. If we have penicillin, we do not need prayer. If we have positive thinking, we do not need the church. If we have manuals on science, we do not need the Bible. If we have an Edison or an Einstein, we do not need a Jesus Christ. They define all of the values of life in material and external terms.

What they do not realize is that the great fundamental need of mankind is redemption and regeneration. What can tractors, machines, manuals of science, and political agencies do with the sin that destroys the human heart and human life? It is to that great human need that the Christian faith addresses itself. The faith of Christ is first and above all things redemptive. It has to do with our sins. How can I be saved from the judgment of God upon the iniquity that characterizes my life?

The Christian faith is by no means an ethic, though it is ethical. It is by no means a theology, though it is theological. It is by no means reformational, though it has social, cultural, and political overtones. The Christian faith is first, fundamentally, and above all a religion of redemption. It has to do with the deliverance of our souls from sin. Christ was delivered for our offenses and was raised for our justification.

One can see this poignantly in the sign of the Christian faith. The sign of the Christian faith is not a burning bush or two tablets of stone. It is not a seven-branched lamp stand or a halo above a submissive head. It is not even a golden crown. The sign of the Christian faith is a rugged and bloody cross. It is a cross with all of its naked hideousness as the Romans would have it. It is a cross with all of its philosophical irrationality as the Greeks would have it. It is also a cross with its power to redeem and to save as Paul preached it.

> Have you been to Jesus for the cleansing pow'r?
> Are you washed in the blood of the Lamb?
> Are you fully trusting in his grace this hour?
> Are you washed in the blood of the Lamb? [1]

The Descent of the Lord from Heaven

The greatest event, the most significant and most dramatic in all of the story of human history is the descent of our Lord Christ from heaven to earth to suffer on the cross. Our minds cannot enter into the immeasurable distance between the heaven of his glory and the shame of his death. Down and down did he come until finally he was made out of the dust of the ground, a man. Among men a slave, the poorest among the poor; executed in the manner of a felon; raised between the earth and the sky as though both refused him; despised by men and rejected by God; cursed and reviled.

As though abuse were not vile enough, they plucked out his beard. As though to pluck out his beard was not contemptuous enough, they pressed on his brow a crown of thorns. As though a crown of thorns were not sharp enough, they drove great nails through his hands and feet. As though the nails did not pierce deeply enough, they thrust into his heart a Roman spear. The crimson of his life poured out of his body onto the ground. Even the sun in the heaven refused to shine or to look upon so tragic and shameful a death.

> Well might the sun in darkness hide,
> And shut his glories in,
> When Christ the mighty Maker died
> For man, the creature's sin.[2]

What is this, the death of our Lord on the cross? What happened? Is it a dramatic play like the *Agamemnon* of Aeschylus, or Shakespeare's *Macbeth* or *King Lear,* or Eugene O'Neill's *Strange Interlude?*

What is this, the death of our Lord? Is it a historical tragedy like Socrates drinking the hemlock or like Julius Caesar murdered at the feet of the statue of Pompey or like Abraham Lincoln assassinated in Ford's Theater?

What is this, the death of our Lord on the cross? Is it a sign of failure, disappointment, and despair? There was a great philanthropist, musician, and theologian by the name of Albert Schweitzer, a doctor who spent the rest of his life in the French Cameroons in West Africa. He was one of the greatest men of all time. He wrote a book entitled *The Quest for the Historical Jesus.* The thrust and summary of that volume is this: The Lord Christ expected the kingdom of heaven to descend apocalyptically. When it did not come Jesus died heartbroken, in frustration, in disappointment, and in despair.

Is that true? Is that the meaning of the crucifixion and the suffering and the sacrifice of the Son of God?

Was it for crimes that I had done
He groaned upon the tree?
Amazing pity, grace unknown,
And love beyond degree! [3]

What is this, the death of the Son of God on the cross? This is God's redemption for our sins. This is the answer to the cry of Job, "[O God,] I have sinned; what shall I do?" (Job. 7:20). This is the answer to the cry of Macbeth: "Will all great Neptune's ocean wash this blood/Clean from my hand? No, this my hand will rather/The multitudinous seas incarnadine,/Making the green one red."

What can wash away my sin?
Nothing but the blood of Jesus;
What can make me whole again?
Nothing but the blood of Jesus.

Oh! precious is the flow
That makes me white as snow;
No other fount I know,
Nothing but the blood of Jesus.[4]

Jesus Is the Atonement for Our Sins

This is the Lamb slain from before the foundation of the earth. This is the blood of the Passover lamb. This is the Suffering Servant of Jehovah by whose stripes we are healed. This is the great redemption of God purposed from before the creation of the world. This is the great climactic moment toward which all time and history did move, when the Lord bowed his head on the cross and cried, "It is finished." The drops of blood in the dust around the cross whispered to the grass, "It is finished." The grass whispered to the herbs, "It is finished." The herbs whispered to the trees, "It is finished." The trees whispered to the birds in the branches, "It is finished." The birds spiraling upward to the clouds whispered, "It is finished." The clouds whispered to the stars, "It is finished." The stars whispered to the angels in glory, "It is finished." The angels in heaven thronged the streets of the New Jerusalem crying to one another, "It is finished." God's great redemptive purpose that we might be saved from our sins has been finished.

This is the sign of our salvation. Wide as the world are the arms of the cross extended eastward as far as the east reaches east, westward as far as the west reaches west, to include all mankind who will pause, who will look, who will trust, who will believe, and who will be saved.

This is the sign of our hope in God and in the world to come. If there is someone loved who is laid in the heart of the earth, there will be a cross at the head of the grave.

> In Flanders fields the poppies blow,
> Between the crosses, row on row.[5]

God forbid that I should glory, save in the cross of our Lord Jesus Christ. Before that great sacrifice, everything else in this life pales and passes away.

Once in a while I think back over the years and years of my life as a minister of Christ. The first funeral that I ever conducted was in a poor community for a tenant couple, poorer than the poor. Their little boy had sickened and died. I was asked to conduct a memorial service. After the service in the little white frame church house, the casket was placed on a truck. The mother sat next to me in my little car, and next to her on the other side was her young husband. As the truck moved down the country road, the mother began to cry inconsolably. The husband put his arm around her and said: "There, there. Do not cry. Jesus will take care of our little boy. He will do it better than we could. We will see him someday in heaven."

After we came to the country cemetery and buried the little form in the casket, as country people do, they heaped up the clods and dirt and made a little mound. Before we left we placed a little cross at the head of the grave. It was a sign of our faith and hope.

There is no other hope. There is no other way. This is God's provision for our salvation and for our redemption in the cross of Christ our Lord.

9
The Blood of Christ

The blood of Jesus Christ his Son cleanseth us from all sin (1 John 1:7).

I have three avowals to make about the text of our message. First, the reference to blood means actual blood. "The blood of Jesus Christ, his Son cleanseth us from all sin." This is no figure of speech, no metaphor, and least of all is it a spiritualization. In a book I wrote some time ago, *Why I Preach That the Bible Is Literally True,* one of the chapters deals with the least effective kind of preaching which is spiritualizing—that is, taking the Word of the Lord and avowing that it does not mean what it says and spiritualizing on it, making it mean whatever a man's imagination might lead him to make it mean.

To me, God-honoring preaching is taking the Word of the Lord and declaring the Scripture just as God said it. A man may not understand all that is in the Bible; he may stagger at its promises; but his assignment and heavenly mandate is to declare and expound the Holy Word of God whether he understands it or not. The Word says *blood* and it means actual blood.

In the days of the apostle John, as in our day, as in all the centuries of Christian history, the faith in Christ has been confronted by the metaphysician and the philosopher who challenge every part of the faith and every advancement that is made in a man's heart. This advancement is made over the violent opposition of the metaphysician, the philosopher, and the unbelieving theologian. For example, in the days of the sainted John there was a Gnostic by the name of Cerinthus who lived in Ephesus. John's Gospel was written in answer, among other things, to Cerinthian Gnosticism. Cerinthus said that Jesus was a man and only a man. He was not deity; he was not God. In answer to that Gnostic heresy the apostle John wrote the Fourth Gospel that Jesus is God: "In the beginning was the Word, and the Word was with God, and the Word was God. The same was in the beginning with God. All things were made by him; and without him was not any thing made that was made. In him was life; and the life was the light of men. And the Word was made flesh" (John 1:1–4,14).

Jesus was God incarnate. John wrote his Gospel against Cerinthian Gnosticism that would state that Jesus was just a man.

The First Epistle of John is written against Docetic Gnosticism. There is no angle at which the mind of Satan does not contrive its confrontation of God's truth in a man's head, in his heart, in his life, in his reading, and in his schooling. One will never go beyond Satan's attempts to trap and ensnare. The Docetic Sophists said that Jesus only appeared to be a man, but that actually he was not a man at all. He was divine, an angel; and he only appeared to be a man. Against that Docetic heresy the apostle John wrote this first epistle. Jesus was a man among men, and he was also God. He was God as though he were not man, and he was a man as though he were not God

The Actual Blood

In his manhood the blood of Jesus Christ is actual blood. "The blood of Jesus Christ his Son cleanseth us from all sin" (1 John 1:7). It is tangible, red crimson that one could touch, could put his hand in the pool of it at the foot of the cross. One could have wiped it with a handkerchief from his brow, from his face, from his hands, and from his feet. One could have caught the blood in a basin as it flowed from his side.

In John 19:34–35 we read: "But one of the soldiers with a spear pierced his side, and forthwith came there out blood and water. And he that saw it bare record, and his record is true: and he knoweth that he saith true, that ye might believe" (John 19:34–35). It is actual blood.

Ask the mother of Jesus. She beheld the agony of her Son. The Lord on the cross said to John, "Behold thy mother" (John 19:27). No woman, no mother should be subjected to such sorrow, tears, and agony as to see her son die like this. The Lord asked John to take her away. John wrote that that moment he took her to his own home. Ask his mother if that was literal, actual blood.

Ask the centurion. He presided over the execution. Ask the soldiers. They nailed his hands and his feet to the tree. Ask the thieves who were crucified on either side of him if it were real, actual blood. Ask the witnesses of heaven in 1 John 5: "This is he that came by water and blood, even Jesus Christ; not by water only, but by water and blood. And there are three that bear witness in earth, the spirit, and the water, and the blood: and these three agree in one" (1 John 5:6,8).

Were you there when they crucified my Lord?
Were you there when they crucified my Lord?
Oh, Sometimes it causes me to tremble, tremble, tremble,
Were you there when they crucified my Lord? [1]

The Blood Is Actually Applied

The blood was not only actual; but it was also

literally offered as an atonement for our souls. One of the magnificent revelations of God from heaven can be found in Hebrews 9:

"But Christ being come an high priest of good things to come, by a greater and more perfect tabernacle, not made with hands, that is to say, not of this building;

"Neither by the blood of goats and calves, but by his own blood he entered in once into the holy place, having obtained eternal redemption for us.

"For if the blood of bulls and of goats, and the ashes of an heifer sprinkling the unclean, sanctifieth to the purifying of the flesh:

"How much more shall the blood of Christ, who through the eternal Spirit offered himself without spot to God, purge your conscience from dead works to serve the living God?

"For when Moses had spoken every precept to all the people according to the law, he took the blood of calves and of goats, with water, and scarlet wool, and hyssop, and sprinkled both the book, and all the people.

"Moreover he sprinkled with blood both the tabernacle, and all the vessels of the ministry.

"And almost all things are by the law purged with blood; and without shedding of blood is no remission.

"For Christ is not entered into the holy places made with hands, . . . but into heaven itself, now to appear in the presence of God for us:

"And as it is appointed unto men once to die, but after this the judgment:

"So Christ was once offered to bear the sins of many; and unto them that look for him shall he appear the second time without sin unto salvation" (Heb. 9:11–14,19,21–22,24,27–28).

He has washed away, expiated, and taken sin away.

All of the high, holy days of the Jewish nation are feast days. Passover is a feast. The Unleavened Bread is a feast. Pentecost is a feast. Tabernacles is a feast. Dedication is a feast. But there is just one fast day. In modern nomenclature it is called Yom Kippur.

In the Bible it is called "The Day of Atonement." On that day the high priest divested himself of his garments of beauty and glory, for he himself was a sinner and a suppliant. He cast lots between two goats, one for Jehovah and one for a scapegoat. The lot that was cast for Jehovah was slain. The high priest took the blood of the sacrifice and, that one time in the year, went beyond the veil and offered the blood as an expiation before God, sprinkling it on the mercy seat. Then the high priest came out from behind the veil, took both hands, and placed them above the head of the other goat and confessed thereon all the sins of the nation. That goat was taken into the wilderness and driven away.

This ritual is a picture and a type, one of God's pictures of how, in the offering of blood, our sins are washed away. We are made clean and white. The author of Hebrews 9 says that were it in a human tabernacle, with a human priest and the blood of goats, the ritual would have to be repeated again and again and again. Each time the ceremony is a remembrance of our sins and a picture of the inefficacy of the human priest, the human offering, and the blood of a goat to wash our sins away. But in the sanctuary, which is in heaven—in this sacrifice, which is that of the Son of God—and in the blood, which is the blood of Jesus Christ—there do we have an offering made one time which suffices for the salvation and cleansing of our souls. As the Jews had a Day of Atonement every year, the Christian had one great Day of Atonement once for all: when our Lord died on a hill called Golgotha, "Calvary." "The blood of Jesus Christ his Son cleanseth us from all sin" (1 John 1:7). It is actual blood, and it was actually offered as an atonement for our souls. Jesus' sacrifice paid all of our debts.

The Blood Provides an Actual Salvation

The shed blood of Jesus provides an actual salvation, a salvation that one can know, feel, and rejoice in forever. The blood offering of our Lord provides a real and an actual salvation in which there is a real and actual substitute. He took our place. He died for us in our stead. We should have died; we should have received that judgment upon our sins. His suffering, sorrow, tears, sobs, and death are vicarious, for us in our stead.

Of all of the people who ever lived, there was no one who had the idea of the atonement of Christ, of his substitutionary death, as did Barabbas. Barabbas was a robber, an insurrectionist, and a murderer. He was imprisoned to be executed by crucifixion according to the Roman practice. One day at nine o'clock in the morning, on a Friday, a Roman legionnaire swung open the iron gates of the prison and called, "Barabbas." The murderer and insurrectionist came to the door expecting to be crucified. Instead, the Roman legionnaire said, "Barabbas, you are free."

Amazed, the insurrectionist walked out to freedom. Just beyond he saw the form of a humble, meek, and lowly man staggering beneath the weight of a heavy cross. When the cross was lifted high, with two of Barabbas' companions nailed to crosses on either side, one can see Barabbas as he elbowed his way through the throng and stood there looking at Jesus, who was nailed on the center cross. He might have said: "That is my cross where I should have died. This man has taken my place." No one could ever have as poignant an understanding of the meaning of atonement as Barabbas.

That is a picture of all of us under the condemnation of sin, judged by the Lord. Jesus died in our stead. He took our place. He is the atoning sacrifice for our sin, an actual substitution.

This Salvation Is Available to the Whole World

The Lord God receives the blood of Jesus as an actual deliverance for our souls. The Lord receives it as an actual pardon, deliverance, and freedom for us. Oh, how God's Book repeats that good news! Paul said that when we were yet in our sins Christ died for us, that in his blood we have peace with God. In Ephesians 2 we read: "That at that time ye were without Christ, being aliens from the commonwealth of Israel, and strangers from the covenants of promise, having no hope, and without God in the world: But now in Christ Jesus ye who sometimes were far off are made nigh by the blood of Christ" (Eph. 2:12–14).

There was a missionary traveling in northern India who came upon a poor, wretched man who had been left by the side of the road to die. The missionary bent over him and said, "Sir, do you have any hope?" The dying man replied, "The blood of Jesus Christ his Son cleanseth us from all sin." When the man spoke those words, he died. The astonished, amazed missionary then noticed that in the closed fist of the dying man was a crumpled piece of paper. He opened the man's hand, removed the paper from his fingers, and saw that it was a page of the first chapter of the first Epistle of John. It bore the words of our text: "And the blood of Jesus Christ his Son cleanseth us from all sin" (1 John 1:7).

God accepts the blood of Jesus as an atonement. Whatever a man may be, God accepts the sacrifice of the Lamb. The Lord says that when he sees the blood, he will pass over you. That dark, awesome night in

Egypt, God said to the believing people (not just Israel, but anybody): "Take the blood of a lamb and strike it on the front of the house in the form of a cross. When the death angel comes to smite the land of Egypt, when I see the blood, I will pass over you" (author's paraphrase). There will be life, not death; light, not darkness; joy, not sorrow; salvation, not wrath; and judgment.

One can easily imagine a man seated in the house under the blood and thinking: "O God, I wonder if my repentance were repentant enough. I wonder if my faith were faith enough. I wonder if my life is good enough. I wonder if my service is acceptable enough. I wonder if I will make it." So many people live in that agony of distress all of their days. If someone asked them if they are saved they would say: "I do not know. Maybe I did not repent right. Maybe I did not believe right. Maybe I did not confess right. Maybe I have not lived right." Oh, what a wretched way to live! God says salvation comes not by your righteousness, not by your repentance, not by your faith, not by your goodness, not by anything in *you*. God says, "When I see the blood, I will pass over you" (Ex. 12:13). The blood of Jesus washes our sins away.

Lord, I could never be good enough. I could never repent enough. I could never have the depth of faith that I ought to have. Lord, Lord, if I am ever saved it is by the grace and mercy of God in Christ Jesus. What I must do is to rest in the promise. "And the blood of Jesus Christ his Son cleanseth us from all sin." So we rest under the blood.

E'er since by faith I saw the stream
Thy flowing wounds supply,
Redeeming love has been my theme,
And shall be till I die.[2]

"Unto him that loved us, and washed us from our sins in his own blood, . . . to him be glory and dominion for ever and ever. Amen" (Rev. 1:5–6).

What a wonderful plan!

What a marvelous promise!

What a Savior!

10
The Crimson Flow

After this, Jesus knowing that all things were now accomplished, that the scripture might be fulfilled, saith, 'I thirst.'

Now there was set a vessel full of vinegar: and they filled a sponge with vinegar, and put it upon hyssop, and put it to his mouth.

When Jesus therefore had received the vinegar, he said, It is finished: and he bowed his head, and gave up the ghost.

The Jews therefore, because it was the preparation, that the bodies should not remain upon the cross on the sabbath day, (for that sabbath day was an high day,) besought Pilate that their legs might be broken, and that they might be taken away.

Then came the soldiers, and brake the legs of the first, and of the other which was crucified with him.

But when they came to Jesus, and saw that he was dead already, they brake not his legs:

But one of the soldiers with a spear pierced his side and forthwith came there out blood and water.

And he that saw it bare record, and his record is true: and he knoweth that he saith true, that ye might believe (John 19:28–35).

In 1 John 5 the beloved apostle again wrote of Jesus: "This is he that came by water and blood, even Jesus Christ; not by water only, but by water and blood. And there are three that bear witness in earth, the spirit, and the water, and the blood: and these three agree in one" (1 John 5:6,8). One cannot read these words without sensing something deeply spiritual in what John was describing.

The crucifixion of our Lord, of anyone, was a horrible thing. There has never been invented a death as agonizing and as tortuous as the Roman custom of crucifying traitors, criminals, and enemies of the empire.

Usually when a man was crucified, he writhed in agony on the cross for a full two or three days. Crucifixion did not destroy in itself any vital organ, so the criminal just hung there until he finally died of exhaustion, which usually took about three days.

Our Lord did not die of exhaustion. He laid down his life and gave up his spirit. So soon did he die, in six hours, that when Pilate heard it he marvelled that Jesus was so soon dead and inquired officially of the centurion who presided over the execution to see whether or not Jesus had thus really expired in so short a time.

The soldiers were brutal and cruel. Their execution by crucifixion of enemies of the state was almost a daily occurrence. They executed slaves, traitors, malefactors, and enemies; and they executed them everywhere and all the time. Such a diverse population as was conquered by the rule of Rome was accompanied by much restiveness, war, and oppression. Judaea was the most restive and rebellious of all. Crucifixion was a common experience, in Judaea and to see men hanging helplessly on crosses was a common sight. The soldiers were adept in murder, in crucifixion, and in execution. The Scriptures say that when they came to look at Jesus, they saw that he was already dead. These hardened men knew when a man was dead; and, looking at Jesus, they saw that he was already dead.

Blood and Water Flowed Mingled Down

To make absolutely sure that Jesus was dead, one of the soldiers took a spear and thrust it into his heart. When he pulled out the spear, out flowed blood and water. So impressive was the phenomenon that blood and water should have poured out of the wound created by the thrust of the spear that John paused to record it.

"The Jews therefore, because it was the preparation, that the bodies should not remain upon the cross on the sabbath day, (for that sabbath day was an high day,) besought Pilate that their legs might be broken, and that they might be taken away.

"Then came the soldiers, and brake the legs of the first, and of the other which was crucified with him.

"But when they came to Jesus, and saw that he was dead already, they brake not his legs:

"But one of the soldiers with a spear pierced his side, and forthwith came there out blood and water.

"And he that saw it bare record, and his record is true: and he knoweth that he saith true, that ye might believe.

"For these things were done, that the scripture should be fulfilled, A bone of him shall not be broken.

"And again another scripture saith, They shall look on him whom they pierced" (John 19:31–37).

What impressed John so deeply that he should write so emphatically about blood and water flowing from the wounds of our Lord? One must look at what John was doing and how he did it to thus see what he meant by his emphasis of blood and water pouring out of the open side of our Lord.

Jesus Taught the People with Signs

When John wrote his Gospel he never used the word *miracle.* There are two words that are constantly used for miracle in the New Testament, especially to describe the marvelous works of our Lord. One is *tera;* that is, "miracle" in the sense of a wonder, "a great amazement," something that had never been seen before. "It was never so seen in Israel" (Matt. 9:33), cried the disciples and the people as they looked at the *tera,* the "wonder" of the works of the Lord. John never used the word *tera.*

Another word for "miracle" is *dunamis*—that is, miracle in the sense of a great manifestation of the power of God that God is able to do such a thing. John likewise never used the word *dunamis,* but he used another word all through his Gospel. He uses the word *semeion,* "sign." What he meant is this. Not only were there spiritual truth and revelation in what Jesus was saying as he taught the people; but there was no less truth, spiritual revelation, in what Jesus did. What he did was a *semeion,* a "sign" that pointed to the truth of God.

The Revelation begins, "The Revelation of Jesus Christ, which God gave unto him, to shew unto his servants things which must shortly come to pass; and he sent and signified it by his angel unto his servant John" (Rev. 1:1). If one pronounced the word *signified* "sign-ified," it would mean more to him. But we change the word to *signified.* "He 'sign-ified' it by the angel unto his servant John." The "sign-ifying" was important to John in the life of our Lord, for what Jesus did was as much an opening, a revelation, of spiritual truth as what he said and what he taught.

For example, in John 2 is presented the miracle of the Lord turning the water into wine. At the wedding in Cana of Galilee there were six large earthenware containers. Each one of them held about three firkens of water—that is, about thirty-two gallons of water. John explained that they were there for the purification of the guests. When the guests arrived, they washed their feet and hands in the containers. When the Lord performed the miracle at the wedding, he asked the servants to fill up all six of the containers. Then he told the servants to bear them to the governor of the feast. When the governor of the feast tasted the water that had turned into wine, he said, "I never tasted wine like this in my life." That is the kind of wine that we shall drink at the marriage supper of the Lamb.

When the Lord instituted the Lord's Supper he said; "I will not drink henceforth of this fruit of the vine, until that day when I drink it new with you in my Father's kingdom" (Matt. 26:29). When John observed that the Lord turned the water into wine, he says that Jesus began using *semeia,* "signs" in Cana of Galilee. What Jesus did was a spiritual revelation. Those six earthenware containers were first filled up. John saw in that sign that in Christ, the law was fulfilled. No jot, no tittle shall fail or fall; but all of the law shall be faithfully kept. The ordinances and judgments that were written against us are all abolished in Christ.

"And bear unto the governor of the feast" the new wine, for this is the new hope, the new promise, the new covenant in the blood and life of our Lord. The Lord did not place wine in an old wineskin that would break; nor did he place a patch on an old garment that would tear. His wine is new. It is glorious, heavenly, from God, a gospel, the good news. When John saw that, it was a sign to him.

Let us look at the feeding of the five thousand. The other three gospels reported the feeding of the five thousand, calling it a "miracle." But not John. He called the feeding of the five thousand a sign. In John 6 we read that Jesus spoke to the multitude the message of the bread of life. Our Lord said: "Verily, verily, I say unto you, Except ye eat the flesh of the Son of man, and drink his blood, ye have no life in you" (John 6:53). What Jesus presented was a sign, a great spiritual revelation.

Jesus Died of a Broken Heart

What sign did John see in blood and water when he said: "I saw out of His side blood and water flow forth. I bear record and I know that my record is true that ye might believe" (author's paraphrase)? It is this: The Lord died of a broken heart, a ruptured heart. In my reading of men who comment on this passage, there are some who will say it was a miracle and inexplicable that blood and water should have flowed out together from the side of our Lord.

In talking to a gifted physician one time, I asked him about the anatomical construction of the human heart and about the death of Jesus. The physician replied: "Around the heart there is a pericardium, the cardiac sac. The heart beats in that sac. It lubricates the heart and keeps it from brushing and throbbing against the lungs. If the heart is ruptured, it will collapse and the blood will pour out into the pericardium. The sac can extend until it covers the entire thoracic cavity. Blood is about 55 percent serum and about 45 percent red coagulum. It can separate. What happened with our Lord was that on the cross his heart broke. When he died the heart collapsed, and the blood gushed out into the pericardium and separated. When the soldier came and thrust his spear through the side into the heart of our Lord, he pierced the pericardiac sac. When he drew out the spear, it was followed by a fountain of blood and water. The crimson and the life of our Lord poured out into the earth."

When John saw that he said, "It is a sign." In the first epistle he wrote of it: "This is he that came by water and blood" (1 John 5:6). The water is a sign of the cleansing, saving gospel grace of the Son of God. It is a sign of the Word that cleanses and saves us. He began his Gospel with the statement: "In the beginning was the Word, and the Word was with God, and the Word was God.

The same was in the beginning with God.

And the Word was made flesh, and dwelt among

us (and we beheld his glory, the glory as of the only begotten of the Father), full of grace and truth" (John 1:1–2,14).

The water is a sign of the cleansing, saving Word, God manifest in the flesh. The Bible speaks of it in John 15:3: "Now ye are clean through the word which I have spoken unto you." In Ephesians 5:26 the apostle Paul said, "That he might sanctify and cleanse it with the washing of water by the word."

The Word of God, the spoken Word, the written Word, the incarnate Word, the Word of God spoken, preached, and delivered always has a salubrious, cleansing, and healthful effect upon the people. There is no man who can hear the gospel of Jesus Christ and not feel somehow that he needs to be washed, to be better, to be saved. That is the water that came forth from our Lord—the saving, cleansing of the blessed gospel message of Jesus!

The Atoning Blood

In 1 John 1:7 we read, "And the blood of Jesus Christ his Son cleanseth us from all sin." The blood of atonement, the blood of expiation, the blood of forgiveness, the blood that covers over and from God's sight and judgment all of the sin of our lives washes us clean and white.

So many of our hymns express how the blood of Jesus washes us pure without spot.

> What can wash away my sin?
> Nothing but the blood of Jesus;
> What can make me whole again?
> Nothing but the blood of Jesus.
> Oh, precious is the flow
> That makes me white as snow;
> No other fount I know,
> Nothing but the blood of Jesus.[1]

In Ephesians 5 Paul avowed that out of the side of our Lord was born the church. He gave an illustration. Just as Eve was taken out of the side of Adam, out of the side of our Lord God took his bride, the church. That is, we are born in his sobs, in his cries, in his tears, in his death, in his cross, and in his sufferings and blood. That is what John saw when he saw the blood and water flow out of our Lord when the Roman spear was withdrawn.

Lord, how is it that we could be so loved of God that Jesus should die for us? "This do in remembrance of me." Bread, his body so torn. Blood, the crimson of his life so poured out that we might live. O blessed gospel of the crimson flow!

11
The Remission of Sins

> And he said unto them, "These are the words which I spake unto you, while I was yet with you, that all things must be fulfilled, which were written in the law of Moses, and in the prophets, and in the psalms, concerning me."
>
> Then opened he their understanding, that they might understand the scriptures,
>
> And said unto them, "Thus it is written, and thus it behoved Christ to suffer, and to rise from the dead the third day:
>
> And that repentance and remission of sins should be preached in his name among all nations, beginning at Jerusalem.
>
> And ye are witnesses of these things.
>
> And, behold, I send the promise of my Father upon you: but tarry ye in the city of Jerusalem, until ye be endued with power from on high."
>
> And he led them out as far as to Bethany, and he lifted up his hands, and blessed them.
>
> And it came to pass, while he blessed them, he was parted from them, and carried up into heaven.
>
> And they worshipped him, and returned to Jerusalem with great joy:
>
> And were continually in the temple, praising and blessing God. Amen (Luke 24:44–53).

The text of the message is: "And he said unto them, Thus it is written, and thus it behooved Christ to suffer, and to rise from the dead the third day: And that repentance and remission of sins should be preached in his name among all nations" (Luke 24:46–47).

This is the gospel; this is our assignment; this is the duty and responsibility of a true preacher of Jesus; and this is the truth held inviolate by the New Testament church. What is our duty, our mandate? It is this: Because Christ suffered for our sins and was raised for our justification, we are to preach the remission of sins to all the nations.

If I am correct in my appraisal, the modern church, as one sees it in the world, proliferated through many denominations, is giving itself to a thousand other interests and enterprises. I do not deny that there are political repercussions in preaching the gospel. I would be the last to say that there are not social ameliorations and reforms that are inherent in the Word of God. I do not contradict the feeling that there are cultural overtones and concomitants that attend the preaching of the message of Christ. But I do avow by the authority of the Lord himself and the Word he spelled out plainly and clearly that our assignment and task is to preach the gospel of the remission of sins.

What is the gospel? Jesus defined it as his death, his suffering and burial, and, on the third day, his resurrection from the dead. On the basis of that atonement and that triumph over sin, death, and the grave, we are to preach the forgiveness of sins. This is also spelled out plainly by the apostle Paul:

"Moreover, brethren, I declare unto you the gospel which I preached unto you, which also ye have received, and wherein ye stand;

"By which also ye are saved, if ye keep in memory what I preached unto you, unless ye have believed in vain.

"For I delivered unto you first of all that which I also received, how that Christ died for our sins according to the scriptures;

"And that he was buried, and that he rose again the third day according to the scriptures" (1 Cor. 15:1–4).

It is possible to address the energies of the church to all of the problems of society—economic, political, social, and cultural. But when the gospel message in the Bible is declared, it addresses itself to the human heart, to the individual soul. Have you been saved? Are your sins forgiven?

The gospel message of Christ addresses itself to the heart. To put new clothes on a man does not make him a new man. To educate a man does not make him a new man. Giving him all of the fine cultural amenities to observe in life will not change his character. The gospel message addresses itself to the man in his soul, in his heart—at the fountain source of his life. It seeks to create in the man a new being. This is the gospel message according to the Word of the Lord.

The Curse of the World

The gospel message, according to our Savior, concerns his death for our sins on the cross and his resurrection from the grave for our justification. The gospel message addressed to the human heart concerns itself with the remission of sin. It has to do with sin. When I hold the Book in my hand and turn through its pages, I find that the whole Bible has to do with sin. The scene opens in the Garden of Eden when the Lord said to our first parents, "In the day that thou eatest thereof thou shalt surely die" (Gen. 2:17). This is the curse of the world.

If one sins against a friend, something dies within him. If one sins against a partner, something will die between them. If one sins against his home, something will die in it. If one sins against himself, something will die in him. When one sins against God, something dies between him and the Lord. When sin is added to anything—to any gift, any virtue, any achievement—it will spell grief and misery and death. A gun plus sin will produce violence and murder. Success plus sin will produce egotism, pride, and overbearing ostentation. Money plus sin will produce greed, bribery, and blackmail. Love plus sin turns to lust. A home plus sin will produce an atmosphere like hell.

Once in a while I will hear a woman lament that she is not married. Apparently there is a biological urge for the sustenance and continuation of the human race without which we would cease to exist. Most women are born with a biological urge to get married. If one of these women does not consummate that marriage, she has the feeling that she has not fulfilled the purpose for which God made her. All of those feelings are perfectly explicable.

If the woman marries the right man, that is great. But if she marries the wrong man, that is hell. It is hell in the morning, and it is hell in the evening. It is hell at noonday and at nighttime, at twilight and at dawn. It is hell as long as they live. You will not have any more of it in damnation and perdition than you will live through right here when you marry the wrong person. That is what sin does. All of those things enter into the destruction of a home.

Alcohol plus sin—a car plus sin—any gift of God plus sin is damned to misery and perdition. God said, "In the day that thou eatest thereof thou shalt surely die." There is a curse in sin.

The Everlasting Stain of Sin

There is an everlasting stain about sin. Sin is in your soul, in your memory, in your heart, in your life, and piece and parcel with you. Sin carries with it an everlasting stain.

In Genesis 49:1 Jacob called his sons and said, "Gather yourself together that I may tell you that which shall befall you in the last days." One of those sons was to receive the blessing. He was to be the one through whom the Messiah was to come. So he turned to his firstborn son. The blessing should have been given to Reuben, but the patriarch said: "Reuben, thou art my firstborn, my might, and the beginning of my strength, the excellency of dignity, and the excellency of power.

"Unstable as water, thou shalt not excel; because thou wentest up to thy father's bed; then defiledst thou it: he went up to my couch" (Gen. 49:3–4).

As Reuben stood there that day at the head of the twelve patriarchal sons of Jacob, he drew himself up to his full height. He was the firstborn; surely the blessing would be his. But Jacob pointed out to him a secret sin that he thought had been forgotten and buried; and it was as livid, as vivid, and as scarlet that day when Jacob looked upon him as on the day when he committed it. Your sins will be that way when you stand before the judgment bar of Almighty God. They were committed in youth, in childhood, in the dark, in secret; but they will be as vivid and livid in the day of judgment as they were the day when you committed them.

If Reuben did not receive the blessing, then the second son, Simeon, should have received it. If he did not, then the third son, Levi, should. Jacob turned to them and said: "Simeon and Levi are brethren; instruments of cruelty are in their habitations.

"O my soul, come not thou into their secret" (Gen. 49:5–6).

What Jacob was referring to is recorded in the Bible and had happened over forty years before. It was a murderous and bloody sin that the two brothers had committed. I would think that Simeon and Levi, as they stood there, thought that what they committed forty years ago had been buried and forgotten in the passing of time. But in the great hour of judgment their sin, too, was as vivid, as livid, and as crimson as the day that they committed it. We do not get beyond the everlasting stain of sin in human life.

The Guilt of Us All

Sin is the common denominator of us all. It is the guilt of us all. The best man in the Old Testament, Job, cried, saying: "I have sinned; what shall I do unto thee, O thou preserver of men?" (Job 7:20). Vice is against society. Crime is against law and order. Sin is against God. That is why in Psalm 51:4 David said, "Against thee, thee only, have I sinned, and done this evil in thy sight." We only sin against God. We violate law. We scorn the law. We disobey all of the perogatives and mandates of men. But sin is against God and God alone.

No need to say to me, "Do not sin." I have sinned. To lecture me about it, to speak to me about it, to ask a reform concerning it has no pertinency whatsoever. I have already sinned.

One time I was driving down a road when a man in a new, flashy, big car passed me rapidly. After a little while I came to a place where the road made a direct right-angle turn. When I got to that turn I stopped the car, for the man in that big automobile, going so rapidly, had been unable to negotiate the sharp turn. On the other side was a bank about waist high. He had driven that car into the bank with a terrific impact.

There happened to be a farmhouse just beyond. When I arrived there I looked at the car. It was blood-splattered. I looked at the man. The farmer and his wife were helping him into the farmhouse. He was badly hurt. There was no need to sit by the side of the man and say: "You ought not to drive fast. Didn't you know that?" The man was hurt and bleeding.

Something needed to be done then. It is the same way with our sins.

One time as a youth I was seated in our house. Across the street were workmen pouring concrete. To my horror, a young man working with the concrete company got his hand caught in the concrete mixer. The cogs were grinding his hand to shreds as it was held in the machinery, and the young man could not extricate it. I stood there and looked at that man and heard his anguish, agony, and cry. No need to go to the side of the man and scold: "Young man, you ought to be more careful using machinery!" His hand was caught in the machine and was an agony of death itself. The same is true about us. No need to come by and lecture that we should be good, nice, fine, and noble.

What I want to know is, what is a message in a word for me when I have sinned? "What shall I do, O thou preserver of men, for I have sinned?" That is the address of the gospel. That is what the Bible is about. The stain in my soul and the sin in my life—is there a remission of sins of which somebody knows? Is there a way of salvation so that, even though I have sinned, I still might see the face of God?

The whole Bible has to do with the remission, the forgiveness of our sins. In the Garden of Eden the Bible tells of forgiveness of sins, beginning with a covering. The Lord slew an innocent animal and poured out its blood, and the earth drank it up. God took skins of an innocent animal which laid down its life to cover the nakedness of our first parents. In the Temple worship the mercy seat was sprinkled with the blood of expiation. The message of the prophets as in Isaiah is: "Come now, and let us reason together, saith the Lord: though your sins be as scarlet, they shall be white as snow; though they be red like crimson, they shall be as wool" (Isa. 1:18). "All we like sheep have gone astray; we have turned every one to his own way; and the Lord hath laid on him the iniquity of us all" (Isa. 53:6).

The ministry of the Lord Jesus is that he shall save his people from their sins. The Lord himself came to give his life as a ransom for many. The blessed installation and introduction of the Lord's Supper is, "This is my blood of the new testament, which is shed for many for the remission of sins" (Matt. 26:28). It is the preaching of the apostle Peter. When the convicted people cried, "Men and brethren, what shall we do?" (Acts 2:37), the reply as recorded in the book of Acts is: "Repent, and be baptized every one of you in the name of Jesus Christ for [because of] the remission of sins" (Acts 2:38). John said, "And the blood of Jesus Christ his Son cleanseth us from all sin" (1 John 1:7). Paul said: "For when we were yet without strength in due time Christ died for the ungodly.

"For scarcely for a righteous man will one die: yet peradventure for a good man some would even dare to die.

"But God commendeth his love toward us, in that, while we were yet sinners, Christ died for us" (Rom. 5:6–8).

This is the glorious apocalyptic revelation: "Unto him that loved us, and washed us from our sins in his own blood, And hath made up kings and priests unto God and his Father; to him be glory and honor and dominion and power for ever and ever. Amen" (Rev. 1:5–6).

"What are these which are arrayed in white robes? and whence came they?

"And I said unto him, Sir, thou knowest. And he said to me, These are they which came out of great tribulation, and have washed their robes, and made them white in the blood of the Lamb" (Rev. 7:13–14).

The message from our Lord himself is that Christ suffered and was raised from the dead and that remission of sins should be preached in his name to all people. That is the good news. That is the message. That is the gospel!

12
His Flesh and Blood

I am that bread of life.

Your father did eat manna in the wilderness, and are dead.

This is the bread which cometh down from heaven, that a man may eat thereof, and not die.

I am the living bread which came down from heaven: if any man eat of this bread, he shall live for ever: and the bread that I will give is my flesh, which I will give for the life of the world.

The Jews therefore strove among themselves, saying, How can this man give us his flesh to eat?

Then Jesus said unto them, Verily, verily, I say unto you, Except ye eat the flesh of the Son of man, and drink his blood, ye have no life in you.

Whoso eateth my flesh, and drinketh my blood, hath eternal life; and I will raise him up at the last day.

For my flesh is meat indeed, and my blood is drink indeed.

He that eateth my flesh, and drinketh my blood, dwelleth in me, and I in him.

As the living Father hath sent me, and I live by the Father: so he that eateth me, even he shall live by me.

This is that bread which came down from heaven: not as your fathers did eat manna, and are dead: he that eateth of this bread shall live for ever (John 6:48–58).

Can you imagine how the people reacted who first heard the words of our text? Ah, what the Lord said is astonishing!

First, I want to point out how the modern preaching of Christ, the Christ of the new theology, the Christ of the new social order, is the Christ for which the people were looking in his day.

In the sixth chapter of John is the story of the feeding of the five thousand. Jesus took the loaves and broke them. Then he took the fishes and broke them until he fed that vast throng. They were gathered on the eastern side of the Sea of Galilee. Then follows the story of the reaction of the people when they saw him. The Lord could feed an army by breaking bread; he could lead them against Rome; he could raise the dead. If the soldiers were killed, he could raise them up. So the people came by force to make him a king, to lead him against Rome, and to bring eternal glory and political splendor to the nation.

The disciples were pleased that Jesus should be king. One of them could be prime minister, one of them chancellor of the exchequer, and another of them chief of staff. But when the disciples began to react in such a way, the Lord sent them away in a boat across the sea. Then he dismissed the throng and went up to a mountain to pray.

Next follows the story of the raging sea and the Lord walking on the water. Then follows the sermon of our text, in the synagogue at Capernaum. When the people tried to find the Lord and could not, they learned that he, following his disciples, had crossed the sea. So they all gathered once again, those thousands of people in Capernaum, pressing inside the large synagogue inside that city. When the Lord saw them he said, "Ye seek me, not because ye saw the miracles [the evidence of the power and presence and saving grace and love of God], but because ye did eat of the loaves, and were filled" (John 6:26).

That is the kind of Christ that is wanted and preached today—a Christ who can bring us material and physical prosperity and well-being. He is the Christ of the social order. If there are sick, in the name of Christ, let us heal them. If there are poor, in the name of Christ let us make them rich. If they are disillusioned and discouraged, in the name of Christ let us pick them up. And let us create a new and a better world for the people.

There are many people in the theological Christian world to whom that kind of a Christ is appealing—one who can feed us and who can bring us material well-being, prosperity, and happiness.

Preach Christ First and All Things Will Follow

One time I heard a missionary state that in Brazil, where he worked, there were so many sick people that he felt he ought to make every effort to get medicines and to minister to their ills. In other areas he saw the people afflicted with malnutrition. The people did not eat correctly, and their diet was nutritionally insufficient. He felt that he ought to turn aside from his missionary endeavors and find food for the people. He would teach them how to eat correctly and be well and healthy. Then he saw people who were in political bondage and needed somebody to guide them in their liberties as citizens of the state; and he felt that he ought to be a social reformer.

But then he learned that these well-meaning services were silent voices to take him away from the great calling he had in Christ. He had been sent by God to save them from sin, to win their souls from damnation and hell. He came to win them to Jesus. These other needs would somehow take care of themselves.

Get a man right with God; get him close to Jesus; make a Christian out of him; and all of these things will follow. But we do not do it that way in our modern day. "Ye seek me not because [of the miraculous presence of God], but you seek me because you did eat of the loaves, and were filled." That is the kind of a Christ the modern day wants. We want comity between nations, comity between individuals, and prosperity and happiness among our people.

The only trouble with that kind of a Christ is that we part with him at the grave. The Lord rebuked the disciples, and he turned to an altogether different kind of word and ministry as he spoke to those people who were looking for a Christ who could bring well-being in this life and make this world a comfortable place to live. He began to speak of the bread of heaven, of eating his flesh and drinking his blood, and of having eternal life in God.

In the text we read: "The Jews then murmured at him, because he said, I am the bread which came down from heaven. And they said, 'Is not this Jesus, the son of Joseph, whose father and mother we know? how is it then that he saith, I came down from heaven?' The Jews therefore strove among themselves, saying, 'How can this man give us his flesh to eat?' Many therefore of his disciples, when they had heard this, said, 'This is an hard saying; who can hear it?' " (John 6:41–42,52,60).

When Nicodemus came to see Jesus, the first thing that the Lord said to that learned ruler of the Jews and doctor of the laws was, "Ye must be born again" (John 3:7). Nicodemus replied: "What, I be born again? Why, I am an old man. How could I enter into my mother's womb and be born again?" (author's paraphrase). What is illogical to man is a fact of truth with the Lord.

In the Gospel of John is told the story of what the Lord said to the woman of Sychar: "You have come to get water out of this well, but the water I could give you would make you never thirst." She said, "By all means, give me that water that I do not come here anymore to the well and draw" (author's paraphrase). Is not that a natural reaction? What an amazing thing for a man to say: "The water that I would give you would make you never thirst."

He Gave Them Bread

The Lord said that the wilderness wanderers were given bread from heaven to eat (talking about Moses and the manna), but said also that "I am that bread of life."

There have been outstanding men who had a great truth, a great message, and a great blessing for the world. Jonas Salk, who discovered the polio vaccine, was a marvelous boon to the world. He developed a method such that all one had to do was take a little wafer or a cube of sugar with a tasteless substance placed on it, and the dreaded disease of polio would be wiped out forever. That is one of the most unusual triumphs in human story. He gave them "bread." I think of Pasteur, who discovered that our diseases were caused by infinitesimal microbes, germs, and bacteria. Ah, think what blessings were these discoveries! He gave them bread; he gave them a great blessing.

But the Lord opens up for us even great foundational blessings. He says, "I am that bread of life." We are to eat his flesh and to drink his blood. When one comes to Jesus he is automatically catapulted into a different world which is not like this world. His life is another kind of life, another kind of thinking. It is the basis for the blessing of all the rest.

One night the Lord was asleep in a boat on the Sea of Galilee with his disciples. He was tired and weary and lay asleep in the bottom of the boat. When a storm came the disciples awakened him. They were in terror, for the boat was about to sink while the Lord was fast asleep. Thereupon Jesus stood up and spoke just a word, and the wind and the waves obeyed his voice. No wonder the disciples said: "What manner of man is this? What kind of a man is this?" One is introduced to another world in the presence of Jesus.

At the tomb of Lazarus the Lord wept and cried just like any other mourner. Then he raised Lazarus from the dead. One cannot imagine such a thing. With Jesus one is in another world.

When the Lord was nailed to the cross and his heart ruptured and the blood spilled out on the ground, he was certainly dead. He was so certainly dead that the Roman soldiers did not even break his bones. They buried the corpse. But the third day he rose again! He is alive! When a man meets the Lord, looks at him, and listens to him, he is in another world. He is in an upward world, a spiritual world, a world where God moves and where God lives.

The same is true with respect to this text. He gave them bread. How many wonderful, blessed men—scientists, doctors, discoverers, business leaders—have blessed the world. "They gave them bread to eat." But Jesus immediately introduces us into an altogether different world, and his new world is the basis for all the blessings that only God can afford. He said: "I am that bread of life . . . and if any man shall eat of this bread, he shall live forever. I will raise him up at the last day."

The Meaning of the Lord's Supper

"Except ye eat the flesh of the Son of man, and drink his blood, ye have no life in you.

"Whoso eateth my flesh, and drinketh my blood, hath eternal life; and I will raise him up at the last day.

"For my flesh is meat indeed, and my blood is drink indeed" (John 6:53–55).

When one reads those words he might think of transubstantiation—the ritualistic Mass—the turning of the bread and the wine into the actual body and blood of Jesus. But these words do not approach transubstantiation. What Jesus said in the institution of the Lord's Supper and what Jesus has said in these verses in John refer to the same great truth. What is said here for our audible ears to hear is portrayed on the communion table for our eyes to see. The truth that the Lord is presenting is two-fold. The first truth is that he was speaking of the sacrifice of his body and atonement for our sins, which is the great moving purpose of God through all of the years and the ages—that in Christ we should be washed clean and white.

John 6 speaks of the Passover season. All the Jews were going to Jerusalem, where the Paschal Lamb was already reserved to be offered and its blood poured out before God. The real Paschal Lamb, whose flesh we eat and whose blood we drink, was to be offered to God. This refers to the sacrifice, the atoning gift of God's love in the body of Christ when he died on the cross.

The second great truth that the Lord was saying is that we appropriate the life of Christ in our hearts and in our lives. We eat of his flesh; we drink of his blood. And what bread is to the nourishment of our human body, so the sacrifice of the body and blood of Jesus is to us in our spiritual lives. We feed upon the Lord, We live in the love, grace, and presence of the blessed Jesus. Our lives are hid with Christ in God. We think of him; we sing about him; we preach about him; we worship and adore him; we ask his loving and guardian care; we pray in his name; we plead his righteousness in the forgiveness of our sins.

We live in the grace and love of Jesus. He becomes a part of our very souls as the bread we eat becomes a part of our very bodies. Search the springs of our salvation and there one will find Jesus. Cut into the heart of our faith and there one will find the blessed Jesus. Look into the secret of this blessed and precious church and there one will find the Lord Jesus. Look into any holy and godly life and there one will find our Lord. How sweet and blessed, how benedictory and precious, is any life that is thus given to God.

A man in days gone by was riding a horse, traveling through one of our Southern states. He came to an old, dilapidated shack; and there in the doorway was an old, stooped Negro woman. The years of hard work had bent her low. Her face was deeply creased, and her hair was as white as snow. The traveler pulled up his horse and, looking down at her in the doorway, said; "Good morning. Do you live here alone?" She lifted up her face to him, and her eyes brightened with a thought. She replied, "Yes, jes' Jesus and me." She lived in a palace! She was the richest old woman in the state! "Jes' me and Jesus."

That is what Jesus meant. A man is poor, ragged, and hungry if he has the whole world and does not know the Lord. But a man is rich; his home is palatial; his life is blessed; and the breath of heaven is the aura and the aroma of the saintliness of his life if he knows and loves the blessed Jesus!

13
Types of Calvary

> Then he said unto them, 'O fools, and slow of heart to believe all that the prophets have spoken:
> Ought not Christ to have suffered these things, and to enter into his glory?'
> And beginning at Moses and all the prophets, he expounded unto them in all the scriptures the things concerning himself.
> And he said unto them, 'These are the words which I spake unto you, while I was yet with you, that all things must be fulfilled, which were written in the law of Moses, and in the prophets, and in the psalms, concerning me.
> Then opened he their understanding, that they might understand the scriptures,
> And said unto them, Thus it is written, and thus it behoved Christ to suffer, and to rise from the dead the third day (Luke 24:25–27,44–46).

In our text we see the marvelous unfolding of the Word of God that Jesus laid before the two disciples on the way to Emmaus. In the latter part of the chapter the Lord opened the minds of the eleven disciples that they might understand the Scriptures. The Scripture expressly says that "beginning at Moses and all the prophets" (and then in the latter part of the chapter of our text, taking the three categories into which the Old Testament is divided—the law, the prophets, and the holy writings—through all of these divisions), the Lord showed them all things concerning himself. That meant that what we read in the Old Testament are types, pictures, outlines, and presentations of the great truth that God would have us learn in Christ Jesus.

One of the most profitable and spiritually rewarding

of all the studies by which one could open his heart to the truth of the Word of God is the study of the types of the Lord in the Old Testament. This is a type:

"And as Moses lifted up the serpent in the wilderness, even so must the Son of man be lifted up:

"That whosoever believeth in him should not perish, but have eternal life" (John 3:14–15).

Why should God have told Moses to take a serpent cast in brass and to lift it up in the midst of the camp? If someone was dying, having been bitten by a little tenuous serpent, he would live if he would look at the brass replica. God was teaching, training, and getting us ready for the great spiritual truth of our salvation in Christ Jesus. Why should the Lord say to Israel (and here is another type): "Tonight the angel of death will visit all the homes in the land of Egypt. But if there is a home that will take the blood of a lamb and sprinkle it in the form of a cross on the lintel and the doorpost on either side, the angel of death will pass over you." To those who were under the blood there was life and salvation, not death and judgment.

That is a type. God did that to teach us what Christ means to us. The purpose of the whole sacrificial system was that we might learn the nomenclature of heaven, that we might understand what God meant when he spoke of an "altar," a "sacrifice," "a propitiatory," an "atonement." The Lord was teaching us what happened when Christ came into the world.

The First Type in the Old Testament

We shall look at the first type and the last type which lay open to view the great spiritual truth of the atoning grace of God in Christ Jesus. The first type in the Bible was:

"And the Lord God caused a deep sleep to fall upon

Adam, and he slept: and he took one of his ribs [side], and closed up the flesh instead thereof;

"And the rib, which the Lord God had taken from man [*bana,* "built," as one would build the temple] made he a woman, and brought her unto the man.

"And Adam said, This is now bone of my bones, and flesh of my flesh: she shall be called [Isha], Woman because she was taken out of [Ish], Man.

"Therefore shall a man leave his father and his mother, and shall cleave unto his wife: and they shall be one flesh" (Gen. 2:21–24).

Let us look now at the New Testament discussion of that type. The apostle Paul had pertinent comments on this subject.

In Ephesians 5 Paul spoke of the church: "Christ also loved the church, and gave himself for it" (Eph. 5:25). In the thirtieth verse he said, "For we are members of his body, of his flesh, and of his bones" (Eph. 5:30). Remember the type, "And Adam said, this is now bone of my bones and flesh of my flesh." The fulfillment of that type is that we are members of his body, of his flesh, and of his bones. Genesis says, "Therefore shall a man leave his father and his mother, and shall cleave unto his wife: and they shall be one flesh." Ephesians says: "For this cause shall a man leave his father and mother, and shall be joined unto his wife, and they two shall be one flesh.

"This is a great [musterion] mystery: but I speak concerning Christ and the church" (Eph. 5:31–32). Paul was very clear about his comparison.

Paul said, "But I speak concerning Christ and the church." This is a type of what God is teaching us in the relationship between Christ and his church. As Eve was taken out of the heart of Adam, from his side, so the church is taken and born out of the riven side of our Lord. We are born in his tears, in his agony, in his cross, in his suffering, in his blood, and in his death.

The Last Type in the Old Testament

The last type in the Old Testament, described and fulfilled in the New Testament, is: "Jesus, when he had cried again with a loud voice, yielded up the ghost, And, behold, the veil of the temple was rent in twain from the top to the bottom" (Matt. 27:50–51).

How meticulously does God stay true to his type! The veil was torn not from the bottom to the top as though men had torn it apart, which is as men would tear it, but from the top to the bottom. It is doubtful that even the strength of men could have torn it, for Josephus says that horses could not have rent that thick and heavy and woven veil. "Behold, the veil of the temple was rent in twain from the top to the bottom; and the earth did quake, and the rocks rent" (Matt. 27:51). The type was made possible in the Old Testament when the Lord God said to Moses: "Thou shalt rear up the tabernacle according to the fashion thereof which was shewed thee in the mount" (Ex. 26:30). Just exactly as God said to do it, so Moses did.

Often I avow that God's people ought to obey the instructions of the Lord just exactly as God has said to. An illustration can be found in our baptismal service. I did not invent the baptismal ordinance. This church did not originate it. John the Baptist said that he was given the form of baptism from God himself. When God revealed its meaning, we learned that baptism means the burial and the resurrection of our Lord, our death with him and our resurrection to a new life in Christ. It is a glorious picture, a promise, a harbinger, and a type of our ultimate, victorious resurrection. We are to baptize as God has shown us.

God's instructions for the creation of the veil were

most explicit: "And thou shalt make a veil of blue, and purple, and scarlet, and fine twined linen of cunning work: with cherubims shall it be made: And thou shalt hang it upon four pillars of shittim wood overlaid with gold: their hooks shall be of gold, upon the four sockets of silver. And thou shalt hang up the veil under the taches [the clasps], that thou mayest bring in thither within the veil the ark of the testimony: and the veil shall divide unto you between the holy place and the most holy" (Ex. 26:31–33). This is God's pattern that he showed Moses from heaven.

Now let us look at the use of the type. In the book of Hebrews we read: "Having therefore, brethren, boldness to enter into the holiest by the blood of Jesus, By a new and living way, which he hath consecrated for us, through the veil, that is to say, his flesh; And having an high priest over the house of God; Let us draw near with a true heart in full assurance of faith." (Heb. 10:19–22).

The author of Hebrews used that veil as a type, and this is the last type used in the Bible. The veil is a type of the flesh of our Lord, the incarnation of our Lord. The glory of the presence of God was veiled with the flesh of Jesus Christ. He was deity, God—and God incarnate, veiled in flesh.

Once in a while one would see the glory of God shining through the physical frame of our Lord, as on the top of the mount of transfiguration. For just a moment, even through the veil of his flesh, the glory of God shone through and the three apostles saw it. No wonder Peter said, "Let us stay here!" It was a glory of glories, seeing God in the flesh. But for the most part, his glory was veiled and the Lord's flesh covered the deity, the shining iridescence, the presence of God. If one had looked upon the Lord, he would have seen a man like other men, made as his brethren. But he was God in the flesh, and the flesh veiled his deity.

It is in the tearing of the veil that we have access into the very presence of the Almighty. As long as the veil was there, as long as Christ was in the flesh, as long as our Lord did not die, we were shut out from God. It is in the tearing of the veil, in the rending of the veil that we have access into the presence of God. Had the Lord remained in his flesh all of his years and had continued to go through all the cities of Israel doing good, to this present day we would still be in our sins. Not by his holy, beautiful, heavenly, celestial, righteous, and perfect life are we saved. It is by his stripes that we are healed.

However beautiful, perfect, and holy the life of Christ may have been; however the veil may have been of blue, purple, and scarlet with inwoven cherubim in the fine twined linen—as long as that veil was there, it shut us out from God. But since the veil was torn, we have had access into the holy of holies. So it is with our blessed Lord. It is in his death, in the rending of the veil that we have boldness to enter into the holy of holies by the blood, the death, the sacrifice of Jesus. Let us then draw near with a true heart in full assurance of faith. Jesus has opened the way in his death in the rending of the veil. He has made an entrance for us into glory. That is the type.

The author of the Hebrews used the type in one other way, one of the most precious of all the interpretations of a type that one could find in God's Book. He spoke of God's promises to us, emphasizing the faithfulness of God. He wrote:

"Wherein God, willing more abundantly to shew unto the heirs of promise the immutability of his counsel, confirmed it by an oath:

"That by two immutable things, in which it was impossible for God to lie, we might have a strong consolation, who have fled for refuge to lay hold upon the hope set before us:

"Which hope we have as an anchor of the soul, both sure and stedfast, and which *entereth into that within the veil;*

"Whither the forerunner is for us entered, even Jesus, made an high priest for ever after the order of Melchisidec" (Heb. 6:17–20).

This type is this: When the veil was torn apart our forerunner, our Lord Jesus, entered in. In his death did he become glorified and immortalized. He entered into glory. Our hope is in that same Lord Jesus, the anchor of the soul, who entered into the veil, beyond the veil, and through the veil. For the Lord made a way for us, and we follow with him into glory.

Ah, what God hath done for us! He has taught us these precious and blessed assurances in the meaning of the death of Christ. God pictured it so that when Christ died, we might understand what he was doing. Oh, the grace, love, and provision for the saving of our souls and the gathering of his chosen, redeemed people into that upper and better world that is yet to come!

14

The Shadow of the Cross

> When Jesus had spoken these words, he went forth with his disciples over the brook Cedron, where was a garden, into the which he entered, and his disciples.
>
> And Judas also, which betrayed him, knew the place: for Jesus ofttimes resorted thither with his disciples.
>
> Judas then, having received a band of men and officers from the chief priests and Pharisees, cometh thither with lanterns and torches and weapons.
>
> Jesus therefore, knowing all things that should come upon him, went forth, and said unto them, "Whom seek ye?"
>
> They answered him, "Jesus of Nazareth." Jesus saith unto them, "I am he." And Judas also, which betrayed him, stood with them.
>
> As soon then as he had said unto them, I am he, they went backward, and fell to the ground.
>
> Then asked he them again, "Whom seek ye?" And they said, "Jesus of Nazareth."
>
> Jesus answered, "I have told you that I am he: if therefore ye seek me, let these go their way":
>
> That the saying might be fulfilled, which he spake, Of them which thou gavest me have I lost none.
>
> Then Simon Peter having a sword drew it, and smote the high priest's servant, and cut off his right ear. The servant's name was Malchus.
>
> Then said Jesus unto Peter, "Put up thy sword into the sheath: the cup which my Father hath given me, shall I not drink it?" (John 18:1–11).

The Lord's betrayal, arrest, trial, and crucifixion were all known to the Lord. "The cup which my Father hath given me, shall I not drink it?" All of his life, even in his preexistent life, Christ lived in the shadow of the cross.

There is a very famous painting of the Lord Jesus in the carpenter's shop. He looks to be a young man about eighteen years of age. The artist has drawn him as he stood doing a carpenter's work. (Tradition says that the Lord made ox yokes and that they were the easiest to bear.) His extended hands caused a distinct shadow to be cast against the wall to his back, and the shadow is that of a Roman cross. In that cross, in its shadow, in its inevitable coming, Christ lived all the days of his life.

Jesus Lived His Life in the Shadow of the Cross

Christ came into this world to die for our sins according to the Scriptures. It is not by his beautiful life that we are saved, but by his suffering and his death. By his stripes, not by his perfect life, we are healed.

The tenth chapter of Hebrews portrays a scene in heaven before the world was made. In that scene the Lord, the Prince of Glory, the Christ of heaven, the preexistent Jesus says that God has prepared a body for him: "For it is not possible that the blood of bulls and of goats should take away sins.

Wherefore when he cometh into the world, he saith, Sacrifice and offering thou wouldest not, but a body hast thou prepared me:

In burnt offering and sacrifices for sin thou hast had no pleasure.

Then said I, Lo, I come (in the volume of the book it is written of me), to do thy will, O God" (Heb. 10:4–7).

Before the age of the ages, before the foundation of the world, before creation itself, in heaven there was a scene in which the Prince of Glory volunteered to die for the creation that should fall into sin and judgment.

When the Lord was presented in the Old Testament prophecies, there was always that overtone of suffering. David in the twenty-second Psalm wrote as though he were standing and looking at the cross. David said: "They pierced my hands and my feet" (Ps. 22:16). David never experienced that, but by prophecy he was describing the cross of Christ.

Isaiah was fully, deeply, and spiritually as accurate as Matthew, Mark, Luke, or John in describing the atoning work of our Savior. The prophet says that upon the suffering servant all of our sins have been laid. "All we like sheep have gone astray; we have turned every one to his own way; and the Lord hath laid on him the iniquity of us all" (Isa. 53:6). He added, "[God] shall see of the travail of his soul, and shall be satisfied" (Isa. 53:11).

When the announcement was made of the birth of the coming king, it was in terms of atonement. "Thou shalt call his name Jesus [Savior]: for he shall save his people from their sins" (Matt. 1:21). When John the Baptist introduced him to his public ministry, it was in those same terms, in that same image: "Behold the Lamb of God, which taketh away the sin of the world" (John 1:29). There was not a Jew who heard that proclamation who did not know its meaning. In the morning he was aware of the morning sacrifice; and in the evening he prayed again at the time of the evening sacrifice. Each time a lamb was slain for the expiation of the sins of the nation. There was no Jew, when he heard that announcement, who did not know that the great, atoning purpose of the coming of Christ into the world was to bear away our sins.

The following great messianic ministry of Christ was lived under the shadow of a cross. In his Galilean tours he took his disciples aside and taught them that he must suffer, die, and be raised from the dead. In his last public appearance in Jerusalem, when the Greeks came to see him, he said, "Except a corn of wheat fall into the ground and die, . . . And I, if I be lifted up from the earth, will draw all men unto me" (John 12:24,32). The coming of the Greeks brought to his heart the memory that he must die for the sins of the world. Even on the glorious mount of transfiguration, Elijah and Moses were speaking to the Lord about his death. They discussed his atoning sacrifice which should be "accomplished" in Jerusalem. The Lord's death had a significant, atoning purpose beyond any other death by which any man ever died in the world.

The institution of the Lord's Supper is a portrayal of his unique death: "This is my body which is given for you. . . . This is . . . my blood which is shed for you" (Luke 22:19–20).

After the trial, there was laid on Jesus a cross. He, bearing his cross, went forth into a place called Golgotha, the place of a skull. There they raised him up beneath the sky and above all the earth, with one malefactor crucified on one side of him and another malefactor on the other side. There on Calvary he died, the central man of all time and eternity, the great Savior, the God-man, Christ Jesus. The whole story of the Bible and the whole burden of the gospel is this: Christ died for our sins according to the Scriptures.

The Shadow of the Cross Has Fallen Across the Entire World

This world could never be the same again because Christ has died in it. The soil of this planet has drunk the crimson blood of the Son of God. We could never forget or escape what Christ has done. There may be other worlds. Scientists sometimes speculate that there are. There may be other planets, other races, other people; but there is none like this earth because the coming of the Christ and the death of our Lord has set aside and apart this planet, this earth from any other part of God's creation in all the stellar universe. How can we forget that it was here that Jesus came, here he died, here his blood was spilled out upon the ground? And here he suffered mental and physical anguish because men would not accept him.

One time soon after the Second World War, I stopped at a British military cemetery in Southern France. I walked through it, looking at the graves of the airmen of the Royal Air Force who had lost their lives in the war. As I walked I saw a wreath on a cross. There was writing on the wreath. These are the simple words that I read: "His wife and his sons will never forget." A British Air Force pilot had lost his life in that dreadful conflict and was buried there. On the cross above his grave, his wife and sons had hung the wreath with the words that they at home could never forget their lost loved one. No one could replace him in their thoughts and their feelings.

We are like that. This is surely the great substance of the message of the Bible, the evangel itself. That is what a man preaches when he preaches the gospel: Christ died in our stead and for our sins. The apostles stood under the shadow of the cross to proclaim the grace of the Son of God, and every sentence and every word that they left behind is stained by his blood. The apostle Paul said, "God forbid that I should glory [that I should boast], save in the cross of our Lord Jesus Christ" (Gal. 6:14).

In the grace and in the preaching of the evangel the cross has become the sin and the aegis of our hope for heaven. If one were looking for a sign of hope, of God, of heaven, and of assurance, one would seek it in our dying Lord. When one sees a cross raised above a fallen form, he knows that somebody there believed in the preciousness, the goodness, and the mercy of Jesus our Lord. The cross of Christ is the sign of our salvation and of our hope of heaven.

All Can Be Saved

The cross is the incomparable invitation of God to the people of the whole world, for the arms of the cross are extended on either side, wide as the world is wide. God presents to us his mercy and grace in the Christ who saves us. In the presence of the death of Christ there are no distinctions—there are no rich and poor, no famous and infamous, no male and female, no bond and free, no black and white. We are all one in the presence of the Son of God.

There was never a more moving story than the one of the Iron Duke of Wellington, who was used of God to save England from the onslaught of Napoleon. England literally worshiped the Iron Duke of Wellington. In keeping with the Episcopal way of worship, he was kneeling at the altar to receive the elements of the Lord's Supper. As he knelt there, a ragged, dirty bum of a man came into the church.

Evidently not knowing who the Duke was, the ragged man knelt by the nobleman's side. The officiating minister, looking at the two men, said to the ragged bum, "Move away. This is the great Duke of Wellington." The Duke, overhearing what the minister said, replied in these words: "Sir, leave him alone. There are no distinctions here. The ground is level at the foot of the cross."

In the arms of the cross, all of us find an equal welcome.

That is so poignantly true when one takes the book of Hebrews and follows the comparison of that God-inspired preacher who spoke of Mt. Sinai with its thunder and its lightning and mount Calvary with its love and grace. So terrible was the sight on Sinai that Moses said, "I do exceedingly fear and tremble." God said, "If any creature shall touch the mount, it shall die."

It was an awesome sight, the God of judgment giving the Ten Commandments. "This do and thou shalt live; disobey, break these commandments, and thou shalt surely die" (author's paraphrase). The God of judgment, of fire, and of wrath spoke on Mount Sinai.

The author of Hebrews then compared the terrors of Sinai with the marvelous grace exhibited on mount Calvary. He said: "For ye are not come unto the mount that might be touched, and that burned with fire, not unto blackness, and darkness, and tempest. But ye are come unto mount Sion, and unto the city of the living God, the heavenly Jerusalem, and to an innumerable company of angels, To the general assembly and church of the firstborn, which are written in heaven, and to God the Judge of all, and to the spirits of just men made perfect, And to Jesus the mediator of the new covenant, and to the blood of sprinkling, that speaketh better things than that of Abel" (Heb. 12:18, 22–24).

Anybody can come to Calvary; anybody can kneel at the cross; anybody can look up to Jesus; anybody can importune his mercy, his grace, and his forgiveness. That is the gospel of the Son of God. The arms of the cross reach out for us all.

PART 3

THE CHRIST—OUR LIVING SAVIOR

And they sung a new song, saying, "Thou art worthy to take the book, and to open the seals thereof: for thou wast slain, and hast redeemed us to God by thy blood out of every kindred, and tongue, and people, and nation;

"And hast made us unto our God kings and priests: and we shall reign on the earth."

And I beheld, and I heard the voice of many angels round about the throne and the beasts and the elders: and the number of them was ten thousand times ten thousand, and thousands of thousands;

Saying with a loud voice, "Worthy is the Lamb that was slain to receive power, and riches, and wisdom, and strength, and honour, and glory, and blessing."

And every creature which is in heaven, and on the earth, and under the earth, and such as are in the sea, and all that are in them, heard I saying, "Blessing, and honour, and glory, and power, be unto him that sitteth upon the throne, and unto the Lamb for ever and ever."

And the four beasts said, "Amen." And the four and twenty elders fell down and worshipped him that liveth for ever and ever (Rev. 5:9–14).

Majestic Sweetness Sits Enthroned

Majestic sweetness sits enthroned
Upon the Savior's brow;
His head with radiant glories crowned,
His lips with grace o'erflow,
His lips with grace o'erflow.

No mortal can with him compare,
Among the sons of men;
Fairer is he than all the fair
Who fill the heav'nly train,
Who fill the heav'nly train.

He saw me plunged in deep distress,
And flew to my relief;
For me he bore the shameful cross,
And carried all my grief,
And carried all my grief.

To him I owe my life and breath,
And all the joys I have;
He makes me triumph over death,
And saves me from the grave,
And saves me from the grave.

—Samuel Stennett

15
Behold the Lamb of God

The next day John seeth Jesus coming unto him, and saith, "Behold the Lamb of God, which taketh away the sin of the world.

This is he of whom I said, After me cometh a man which is preferred before me: for he was before me.

And I knew him not: but that he should be made manifest to Israel, therefore am I come baptizing with water."

And John bare record, saying, "I saw the Spirit descending from heaven like a dove, and it abode upon him.

And I knew him not: but he that sent me to baptize with water, the same said unto me, Upon whom thou shalt see the Spirit descending, and remaining on him, the same is he which baptizeth with the Holy Ghost.

And I saw, and bare record that this is the Son of God."

Again the next day after John stood, and two of his disciples;

And looking upon Jesus as he walked, he saith, "Behold the Lamb of God."

And the two disciples heard him speak, and they followed Jesus (John 1:29–37).

John the Baptist was a man born to say one sentence. His ministry was meteoric, for he arose out of the barren desert wastes of the wilderness of Judea, delivered his message, and almost as quickly disappeared from the scene of spiritual history. He was born to say one sentence, the sentence that was the introduction to the world of the Son of God, Jesus Christ. John's introduction was the beginning of the public ministry of our Lord.

Had you been that elect forerunner sent into the world to introduce Christ, what would you have said?

There are those who would have introduced the Lord with this wondrous exclamation: "Behold a man who can raise the dead." Every newspaper reporter on the earth would have delighted in that caption. Others might have said, "Behold a man who can feed the poor!" It seems as though the United States of America has a complex about people who will not work, those who do not care, and those who do not help themselves. They call upon the other part of America that is working to support those who will not work, will not try, and will not help themselves. It is a wonderful thing to help people who are deserving, who try, who work, and who, because of ill fortune, fall into sickness or poverty beyond their control. But we have a guilt complex in America that sends us into ten thousand welfare programs that become increasingly more inane as they are implemented in the cities, counties, and governments of America.

Others might say: "Behold a man who can call legions of angels!" One time the Lord said all he had to do was to say the word and 72,000 would be there by his side, fighting in behalf of the cause and comfort and deliverance of the Son of God. Only one angel came down out of God's heaven and passed over the army of Sennacherib's Assyrians. The next morning when Jerusalem and Hezekiah awakened out of their sleep, there were 185,000 corpses. The entire army of Sennacherib was dead. Just one angel! Think of having 72,000.

Here is a man who can heal the sick. He can open the eyes of the blind. He can still the tempest and calm the storms. Just think of how enthusiastically the reporters would write about him and how people would introduce him! I can just see their dramatic imaginations as they present the towering, glorious Son of God.

The Lord raised up the great Forerunner, John the Baptist, and sent him into the world to say this one introductory sentence: "Behold the Lamb of God, which taketh away the sin of the world."

The Sin of the World

God says that what is the matter with this world is not its poverty, disease, suffering, death, blindness, crippledness, or greed. God says that what is the matter with the world is the sin that lies back of all of the judgments of suffering, disease, horror, violence, bloodshed, and death.

As David Livingstone in East Africa watched those endless Arab trains of slaves, he said, "God's blessing be upon any man, American, Englishman, or Turk who will help to heal this open sore of the world." I think of that as God looks upon this earth, the affliction by which we are troubled and the curse by which we are plagued.

Men are returning to some of the old doctrines in the Bible that our forefathers preached and at which the psychologists and sociologists of this past generation used to scoff and laugh. We are becoming increasingly more aware that the problem with which we cope and the monster against which we battle is just as it was described in the Bible by the old-time preachers. They called it the doctrine of total depravity: We are born sinners. That is not the doctrine that a man is as vile and evil as he can be, but it is the doctrine that sin has entered every faculty and every emotion of our fallen natures. Unless a man is disciplined, he becomes increasingly evil.

A distinguished judge in one of the courts of America in an interview from a report of the Minnesota Crime Commission said: "The best pronouncement on this subject of what is the matter with us today is to be found in a report of the Minnesota Crime Commission. The report says: 'What we call delinquent behavior is as old and universal as man. It is not something to which only an evil or moronic segment of humanity, different from the rest of us, is liable. It must be remembered that no infant is born a finished product. On the contrary, every baby starts life as a little savage; is equipped, among other things, with organs and muscles over which he has no control, with an urge for self-preservation, with aggressive drives and emotions like anger, fear, and love, over which, likewise, he has practically no control. He is completely selfish and self-centered. He wants what he wants when he wants it—his bottle, his mother's attention, his playmate's toy, his uncle's watch. Deny him these wants and he seethes with rage and aggression which would be murderous were he not so helpless.

"He is dirty. He has no morals, no knowledge, no skills. All children are born delinquent and, if permitted to continue in the self-centered world of his infancy, given free rein to his impulsive actions to satisfy his wants, every child will grow up a criminal, a thief, a killer, and a rapist. In the process of growing up, it is normal for every child to be dirty, to fight, to grab, to steal, to tear things apart, to talk back, to disobey, to obey. Every child has to grow out of delinquent behavior.'

"What we need is discipline!"

When men face facts as facts are and face reality as reality is, any man conversant with human nature will finally come to that conclusion: Men are born depraved. There are emotions and feelings of depravity that all of us feel. God calls it sin. That is our problem and the problem to which God addresses himself.

Nothing in itself is wrong. God says so in Romans 14:14: "I know, and am persuaded by the Lord Jesus, that there is nothing unclean of itself."

There is nothing inherently wrong with alcohol. In

fact, there could be no practice of medicine without alcohol, the solvent in which so many of our medicines are carried. Alcohol is an effective antiseptic and cleansing chemical. But when alcohol is combined with sin, one falls into all kinds of disaster. The drunks, as well as the people who make money off the weaknesses of humanity, commit sin.

There is nothing wrong with playing cards, dominoes, or games. It is when one adds sin to it, gambling, that he falls into the same depraved disaster.

A gun is one of the finest instruments in the world. But add sin to it and one has blood, murder, and blackmail. God deals not with the pimples on the surface but with the bloodstream and the heart. The problem is not the gun, the needle, the cards, or the movie. The problem is the sins to which they become wedded. Take a gun from a murderer and he is still a murderer because the desire to murder is in his heart. Take the bottle away from the drunkard and he is still a drunkard because the desire to drink is in his heart. Take the needle away from the dope addict and he is still a dope addict because in his heart he wants dope.

In Memphis, Tennessee, I talked to a godly couple who had picked up a young harlot out of the gutter and had nursed her back to health. They had cleaned and dressed her up and had taken her to live with them. They said that to their great sorrow, the girl slipped out of the house at night and returned to those dens and dives of harlotry and prostitution. Is not that an astonishing thing?

There is not anything in itself that is wrong. Our problem is not out there somewhere, but our problem is inside. That is why John presented his tremendous introduction of the Son of God: "Behold the Lamb of God, which taketh away the sin of the world."

God works in wonderful ways. Wherever there is a poison, there is always an antidote. God put it together.

I once read that in the Bahamas there was a Negro boy who, fleeing from a rainstorm, found refuge under a tall bush. As the rain fell on the bush, the water dripped down from the leaves onto the boy. The poison from the bush entered the pores of his skin, and he died. A doctor in America heard about the case and went to the Bahamas to seek out the unusual situation. The physician found by talking to some of the old tribal chieftains that wherever that bush grows, there is another bush close by. One can take the leaves of the second bush and rub them on the surface of the skin, and the poison from the first bush is washed away. In reading of that experience I thought of Revelation 22:2: "And the leaves of the tree were for the healing of the nations." Every bottle of poison has an antidote.

God provided Jesus as the antidote for our sin!

God Provides a New Way, a New Heart, and a New World

How does it work? "Behold the Lamb of God, which taketh away the sin of the world." He took our penalty and our judgment. Jesus took all of the wrath and judgment of God on our iniquity and bare it on the tree. In our acceptance of that atoning grace, the Holy Spirit does something inside of us. He washes the stain of sin out of our souls. He forgives all our iniquities. He creates in us a new heart, a new love, and a new life.

Not only in this life, but in the life that is to come, Jesus goes with us. When the Lord died and entered into heaven, did he go alone? Was he by himself when he went back to the Father? When he went into glory he went arm in arm with the thief who died by his side on the cross. "The Lamb of God who takes away the sin of the world." Think of being a John the Baptist pointing the way to Jesus and eternal life!

One time when I was preaching in Florida I received a telephone call from a man in Mississippi who said: "You do not know who I am. I am calling for a young wife here in our city. Her husband was an electrical engineer. The two lived in the city of Dallas. In your study at the church you won that young engineer to Jesus and baptized him. While doing an assignment here in a city of Mississippi, as the man was working, something went wrong and he was electrocuted and killed. The first thing his wife wanted to do was to call you. I am doing it for her. She wanted to tell you that the sweetest and most comforting assurance in her heart is the remembrance of that day when you won her husband to the Lord."

There is no reward compared to the rewards that God gives a man who will stand as an emissary from heaven and point to the Lamb of God that taketh away the sin of the world. That is what John did, and that is what we are doing today!

16
"Ecce Homo!"

> Then came Jesus forth, wearing the crown of thorns, and the purple robe. And Pilate saith unto them, "Behold the man!" (John 19:5).

The exclamation of Pontius Pilate, the Roman procurator, as he brought Jesus out of the judgment hall and set him on a balcony above the people, where the maddening crowd could see him, is a theme of artistry and poetry and a sermon in itself. *"Ecce homo!"* is translated "Behold the man!"

History will say that no small part of the means and reason for the death of one who was crucified lay in the scourging, for the Roman soldiers almost beat the life out of the one who was to be executed. The first verse of John 19 says that Pilate took Jesus and had him scourged. He was a bloody mass.

With the crown of thorns pressed on his brow and the blood coming down His face, the Lord stood there with a cast-off purple robe, which the soldiers had found somewhere in the palace and had placed around his shoulders. For a scepter they placed in his hand an ugly reed. Bowing down before him, they cried, "Hail, King of the Jews!" (Matt. 27:29). The Romans would do anything to show contempt for the hated and despised Jew.

While the Roman soldiers were mocking and ridiculing the Lord, apparently Pontius Pilate happened to walk through the judgment hall once again and looked upon the innocent man covered in blood, an object of contempt and ridicule. Seeking to release the Lord, he was somehow moved with pity and compassion by the spectacle of the suffering Christ. Seeing him thus bruised, mutilated, beaten, and ridiculed—an object of scorn and contempt—Pilate thought that the same feeling of pity and compassion that had moved his heart would also move the hearts of the throng on the pavement below.

He took the Lord and stood him there at the front of the balcony and said those famous words, *"Ecce homo!"* So full of amazing meaning and pity has been that sight that artists for centuries have painted the picture of Christ with the crown of thorns, bloody and beaten, suffering, preparing now for his crucifixion and his execution, standing there before the crying throng who are asking Pilate for his blood, his life, his crucifixion.

As we ourselves look upon that scene, it is startling in the extreme and astonishing beyond measure. "Behold the man!" Look at him, the crowned prince of glory in heaven before the world was made, for this is none other than the manifestation of God in the flesh. The Scriptures expressly state: "In the beginning was the Word and the Word was with God, and the Word was God. All things were made by him; and without him was not any thing made that was made.

And the Word was made flesh, and dwelt among us, (and we beheld his glory, the glory as of the only begotten of the Father,) full of grace and truth" (John 1:1,3,14).

This is God manifest in the flesh. The apostle Paul said, "For in him dwelleth all the fulness of the Godhead bodily" (Col. 2:9). The author of Hebrews said, "Who being the brightness of his glory, and the express image of his person" (Heb. 1:3). This is the Creator of all the universe and of all the worlds. Paul said:

"Who, being in the form of God, thought it not robbery to be equal with God:

"But made himself of no reputation, and took upon him the form of a servant, and was made in the likeness of men:

"And being found in fashion as a man, he humbled himself, and became obedient unto death, even the death of the cross [the death of a slave, of a malefactor]" (Phil. 2:6–8).

"Behold the man!" Think of him, in glory, the prince of heaven, God himself. The contrast is unbelievable and astonishing. Meek, bloody, crowned with thorns, prepared for execution and death. Behold the man!"

Look at the startling contrast of the nativity and the incarnation in Bethlehem, the first Christmas night. Think of how the angels sang and how the shepherds adored and worshiped! What a beautiful, glorious night of nights when the heavens turned to the praise and glory of God, for the Word had become flesh. God had appeared in human form, and the preincarnate, theophanic Christ now was in the earth. Bethlehem's manger held the Christ child, the Son of God. Oh, what a night of nights, what a happiness, what a glory, what a gladness. But now, "Behold the man!" Bloody, beaten, crowned with thorns, ridiculed, despised, and scorned.

When he was brought to the Temple as a child, Simeon the aged prophet said to his mother Mary, "Yea, a sword shall pierce through thy own soul also" (Luke 2:35). Standing at the foot of the cross, his mother watched him crucified. "Behold the man!" What a startling, astonishing contrast!

Look at Our Lord in His Saving Ministry

Think of him in his ministry—the lowly, humble Jesus going about preaching the gospel to the poor, doing good, healing the sick, opening the eyes of the blind, unstopping the ears of the deaf, cleansing the lepers, raising the dead—the sweet, gentle, and lowly Jesus. Bloody, beaten, outcast, despised, rejected, and now prepared for crucifixion and death. What a contrast that so lovely and beautiful a life should end in such suffering and death!

There has never been a tragedy in human history like the tragedy of the crucifixion of Jesus. There has never been such an indictment and judgment upon the fallen human race such as that! What God gave to us in Bethlehem we handed back to him on the point of a Roman spear, crucified like a malefactor, like a criminal. How could such a thing be? From where did such tragedy come? Who did it? Whose guilt is this? The innocent, lowly, precious, and gentle Jesus, beaten, thorn-crowned, and dying—who did that? Who nailed him to the cross? Who pressed on his brow that crown of thorns? Who scourged him unto death?

Who Is Guilty of the Death of Christ?

There are many answers. There are those who would say God did it. Is not he responsible for all things in the earth? Does he not reign as king over all heaven and earth? God did it. That is what Job's wife said to him when he fell into such sorrow and distress. Job's wife said to him, "Curse God, and die" (Job 2:9). God could change the conditions of the world if he wished. He could take away sin, war, death, and suffering if he chose. It is God's fault.

There are those looking at Jesus saying: "He did it himself. It is his own fault, he got himself into that trap; he maneuvered himself into that corner. He made his own bed; let him lie in it. He should have been smarter and shrewder."

There are those who say Pontius Pilate did it. He

crucified Jesus. Pontius Pilate could have liberated him, but Pontius Pilate was a spineless judge with no courage or character. Pontius Pilate did it.

There are those who say the Jews did it. They delivered him to crucifixion and to death. They are the ones who accused him, who brought him to the judgment.

There are those who say Judas did it. He is the one who sold him for thirty pieces of silver. He is the one who brought the soldiers and the Temple officers to arrest him that night. It is Judas' fault.

There are those who say the Roman soldiers did it. Crucifixion was a Roman institution. Who drove those nails in his hands? The Roman soldiers. Who pierced him with a spear? The Roman centurion. Who gambled for his garments? The Roman soldiers.

You know, I can hear each one of those standing before the judgment bar of God and saying, "It is not our fault."

Have you ever been to Lucerne, Switzerland, one of the most beautiful cities of the world, and Lucerne Lake, one of the most beautiful lakes of the world? Across from Lucerne is Mount Pilatus, Mount Pilate. The first time I was there I asked, "Why would they name that Mount Pilate?" The answer was very plain and much in tradition. When Pontius Pilate was dismissed from his procuratorship, his governorship, he was sent in exile. He committed suicide, and they buried his body in Lake Lucerne. Tradition has said that through the centuries Pontius Pilate in the twilight of every evening rises from the bottom of the lake and washes his hands in the pure blue waters of Lake Lucerne. He cries, saying, "I am innocent of the blood of this man; I wash my hands; it is not my fault."

The Jews to the last one of them would say: "We are innocent of the blood of this man. Do not bring his blood upon our heads and upon the heads of our children."

The Roman soldiers without fail would stand and say: "We were but men under authority. We were executing the commands of our centurion and of the Roman procurator."

At the judgment bar of Almighty God I think we will all stand and confess and admit and truthfully avow, "We all did it." Our hands pressed upon his brow the crown of thorns. Our hands nailed him to the tree. Our hands thrust into his side that iron spear. Our sins brought about the death of the Son of God. We all did it.

Our Repentance

There has never been a group of missionaries like the Moravians, who brought John Wesley to the saving knowledge of Christ. It was the Moravians who inspired the Baptist missionaries, beginning with William Carey. The Moravians were the frontiersmen to the ends of the earth under the Arctic Circle in the north, under the steaming jungle sun in the south, to the ends of the continents, and to the isles of the sea. From where did they come?

In southern Germany a young nobleman reigned over a large kingdom. His name was Count Zinzendorf. He was a good-looking, swashbuckling, happy-go-lucky young man. He was also a nobleman, a rich man, a handsome man; and he was living it up. One day while walking through the art gallery in Düsseldorf he suddenly stood transfixed. This young man of the world stood riveted in attention. What had caught his eye? An *Ecce Homo,* a picture of the Son of God standing before a bloodthirsty throng, crowned with thorns, the blood flowing from his face and his back, sorrowfully looking down upon those who stood in front of that picture. Underneath was the caption in Latin, *"Hoc feci pro te; quid facis pro me?"* ("This have I done for thee; what hast thou done for me?") And the young count turned, walked out of that Düsseldorf gallery, went back to his house, and gave himself, his kingdom, his life, and his wealth for the evangelization of the world. "Behold the man!"

Do you feel like that when you picture the Son of God dying? Does the Holy Spirit take the message of its love, grace, and mercy and press its appeal to your heart? Does he? I have felt that since a child, I could not tell you the number of times that I sat as a boy in a congregation and listened to the preacher tell about the death of Jesus when I just sat there and cried, moved by the love of God in the Lord.

I still am so moved. It would be very difficult for me to listen to a man preach about the death of Christ and not feel something in my soul. *"Hoc feci pro te; quid facis pro me."* "This have I done for you; what hast thou done for me?"

17
What Shall I Do with Jesus?

When he was set down on the judgment seat, his wife sent unto him, saying, "Have thou nothing to do with that just man: for I have suffered many things this day in a dream because of him."

But the chief priests and elders persuaded the multitude that they should ask Barabbas, and destroy Jesus.

The governor answered and said unto them, "Whether of the twain will ye that I release unto you?" They said, "Barabbas."

Pilate saith unto them, "What shall I do then with Jesus which is called Christ?" They all say unto him, "Let him be crucified."

And the governor said, "Why, what evil hath he done?" But they cried out the more, saying, "Let him be crucified."

When Pilate saw that he could prevail nothing, but that rather a tumult was made, he took water, and washed his hands before the multitude, saying, "I am innocent of the blood of this just person: see ye to it."

Then answered all the people, and said, "His blood be on us, and on our childen."

Then released he Barabbas unto them: and when he had scourged Jesus, he delivered him to be crucified (Matt. 27:19–26).

There is not a more fundamental or primary question that the whole world faces than this: "What shall I do with Jesus, who is called Christ?" The questions of government, of state, of business, of civic community and leadership, of family, of individual soul is: What shall I do with Jesus, who is called Christ?

What shall I do with his words? "Never man spake like that man." Such words did he say: "I am the way, the truth and the life: no man cometh unto the Father but by me" (John 14:6). "He that hath the Son hath life: and he that hath not the Son hath not life" (1 John 5:12). What shall I do with his words?

What shall I do with his life? "It was never so seen in Israel" (Matt. 9:33). There was never a life like that. Not only in the days of his flesh, but through the continuing centuries and down to this present hour does the living Lord speak to us. He confronts us on every Damascus road. He demands of us the highest in every decision we make. What shall I do with his life?

What shall I do with his death? The death of our Lord was the only death in the world that is substitutionary for the sins of our souls. "This is my blood of the new testament which is shed for many for the remission of sins" (Matt. 26:28). No man ever died for the sins of the world but that man. What shall I do with his death?

What shall I do with his resurrection? He was raised from the dead for our justification that in him we might have hope of heavenly and eternal righteousness. What a glorious hour when the pastor can stand at a memorial hour of a sainted member of the church and say, "This man is with the living Lord." It was Christ Jesus who said: "I am he that liveth, and was dead; and, behold, I am alive for evermore, and have the keys of hell and of death" (Rev. 1:18). What shall I do with his resurrection?

What shall I do with his promised return? Not forever will this world continue in its sin and iniquity. Not forever shall death reign among men. Not forever shall our hearts be filled with tears of agony, struggle, and trouble. Someday there shall be an intervention from heaven when Christ comes down. "Behold, he cometh with clouds; and every eye shall see him, and they also which pierced him: and all kindreds of the earth shall wail because of him" (Rev. 1:7).

Pilate's Five Evasions of Jesus

In the story of the trial of Jesus before Pontius

Pilate, there are five evasions of that Roman procurator as he wrestled with the problem of what to do with Jesus. However he turned, that problem came back to him again—just as it does with us.

First, Pilate, upon learning that Jesus was from Galilee, another unit in the Roman Empire under the jurisdiction of Herod Antipas, sought to rid himself of the problem of facing the Lord by sending him to Herod. "If Herod condemns him, I will condemn him. If Herod frees him, I will free him. If Herod accepts him, I accept him. I will do what Herod does."

How many times do I see that in the lives of people? "I will do what he or she does. I will do what the crowd does." We are like people who have no will and no volition of our own. We do what is for the moment popular, expedient, or acceptable. But always and inevitably that question comes back to us: What shall *I* do with Jesus?

I have to breathe for myself. One day I shall die for myself. There is no one in the earth who can die for me. Someday I shall be judged for myself. There are great moments in every man's life when he stands naked and alone before God. This is one of them. What shall I do with Jesus, who is called Christ?

Pilate's second evasion was: "Let us compromise. Let us not decide one way or the other. I will scourge him, and then we will let him go."

How many times do I see that in the lives of our people? "I will not follow him; nor will I give my life to him. What I will do is give up this and forsake that and turn away from another thing. I will do this much and that much. I will not give myself wholly to the Lord, but I will compromise. I will try to do better."

Third, Pontius Pilate tried to reason with that angry and infuriating throng. Pilate brought Jesus out, a pitiful figure—crowned with thorns, beaten, a mock purple robe upon him, and a reed in his hand for a scepter. Thinking somehow that he could reason with that mob crying for Christ's blood and life, Pilate brought Jesus out on the balcony and said, "Behold the man" (John 19:5). He meant: "Look at him. One would not demand the life and blood of someone like that."

One does not reason with Satan. Satan demands an absolute repudiation of the Son of God. There is no sympathy in Satan for the Prince of Glory. He demands his crucifixion. He demands his rejection. He says, "Do not go down the aisle and accept him as your Savior." He can give you a hundred reasons why not, and a thousand other reasons why not now. No one of us is an equal for Satan. We cannot out-think him, and we cannot out-reason him. Even Michael the archangel cowered before Satan. How much less are we able, we who are made out of dust and ashes? When one starts listening to Satan, he is lost.

The fourth evasion of Pilate was in a mode of substitution. Let us substitute something else. Pontius Pilate said, "Let us substitute Barabbas." Barabbas was a villain, a murderer, and a traitor. He was guilty of treason and had been sentenced to die. Pilate gave them the choice of Barabbas or Jesus. He thought the people would say, "Let us destroy Barabbas." Pilate's hope was in this substitution.

How often do I see that? "I will not accept the Lord, but I will substitute something for him. I will live a good life. I will pay my honest debts. I will walk as a noble citizen." A man will substitute some other way or persuasion—anything except humbly and preciously, prayerfully and believingly, to let Jesus come into his heart.

In the little country church where I once pastored,

there was a man who was a chain smoker. He developed a little sore on his lower lip from which a cigarette always dangled. The sore did not go away, so he went to the county seat and asked the physician about the sore. The physician looked at it and said: "You have a cancer on your mouth that is very serious. Go to such and such a city and go to such and such a hospital and go to such and such a surgeon. You must have the sore removed because it is dangerous."

The man returned home, and his neighbors learned of the cancer on his lower lip. One of his dear friends came to him and said: "It is expensive to go to the city. It is more expensive to go to the hospital. It is still more expensive to pay the fee of a surgeon. I have a little vial of medicine at home. I will bring it to you. You put the medicine on the sore, and it will heal the sore forever." He took the medicine and placed it on the sore.

The days and weeks and months passed, and the man went back to the physician. By that time the sore had worsened. The physician looked at him and said, "Sir, are you not the man to whom I said, 'You have a cancer. Go to the hospital'?" The man said, "Yes." The physician said, "Why did you not go?" The man replied, "Doctor, a neighbor said that if I would use this little vial of medicine, it would heal the cancer and save me the time and expense." The day came when that cancer ate away the entire lower part of his face and neck, and his tongue lay on his chest.

That is exactly what Satan does to us when the Holy Spirit points to the Son of God. We are afflicted people. We are dying people. We are sinful people. Sin is not only a wrestling in this life, but it has to do with the judgment that is to come. When I stand at the great bar of Almighty God, what shall I do with my sins? Satan comes and has all kinds of suggestions—when what we need is the Great Physician who can heal us and who can save us.

The fifth invasion of Pilate was the most tragic of all. The governor called for a basin of water and a towel. There before the great throng he washed his hands. He dried them with a towel and said: "I am innocent of the blood of this just person: see ye to it" (Matt. 27:24). But he delivered Jesus to be crucified! There is no neutrality facing God and facing Jesus.

No man can escape this ultimate and final question: Shall I crown or crucify Jesus? Shall I accept or reject him? Shall I love or refuse him? Shall I follow or disown him? Shall I give him my heart and life, or shall I keep it for myself? What shall I do with Jesus, who is called Christ?

18
"It Is Finished"

Then the soldiers, when they had crucified Jesus, took his garments, and made four parts, to every soldier a part; and also his coat: now the coat was without seam, woven from the top throughout.

They said therefore among themselves, "Let us not rend it, but cast lots for it, whose it shall be": that the scripture might be fulfilled, which saith, "They parted my raiment among them, and for my vesture they did cast lots." These things therefore the soldiers did.

Now there stood by the cross of Jesus his mother, and his mother's sister, Mary the wife of Cleophas, and Mary Magdalene.

When Jesus therefore saw his mother, and the disciple standing by, whom he loved, he saith unto his mother, "Woman, behold thy son!"

Then saith he to the disciple, "Behold thy mother!" And from that hour that disciple took her unto his own home.

After this, Jesus knowing that all things were now accomplished, that the scripture might be fulfilled, saith, "I thirst."

Now there was set a vessel full of vinegar: and they filled a sponge with vinegar, and put it upon hyssop, and put it to his mouth.

When Jesus therefore had received the vinegar, he said, "It is finished": and he bowed his head, and gave up the ghost (John 19:23–30).

There are seven sayings from the cross. The first one is: "Father, forgive them; for they know not what they do" (Luke 23:34). The second one is: "To day shalt thou be with me in paradise" (Luke 23:43) The third one is: "Woman, behold thy son! [and son,] Behold thy mother!" (John 19:26–27). The fourth one is: "My God, my God, why hast thou forsaken me?" (Mark 15:34). The fifth one is: "I thirst" (John 26:28). The sixth one is: "It is finished" (John 19:30). The seventh one is: "Father, into thy hands I commend my spirit" (Luke 23:46).

Read over the sixth saying from the cross. "It is finished." What is finished? The great purpose for which our Savior came into the world, that he might make atonement for our sins. Jesus was a volunteer in glory when the Lord God, first seeing the fall of the human race, searched the ramparts of heaven for someone who was worthy to open the seals that contain the names of the redeemed of the Lord. Search was made in heaven, in the great planetary systems, in the nether world in the abyss below; and there was none worthy. When no one was able to deliver the fallen race, there appeared the Son of God, the Prince of Glory. He volunteered to give his life a ransom, an atonement, an expiation, a payment for the debt of sin that the human race owed before God. This is the purpose of his coming into the world. All of the facts of the Old Testament, all of the furniture in the sanctuary, and all of the sacrifices pointed toward that one great consummating moment when the Son of God should die for the sins of the world.

The Lord's Death

Let us reverently look upon the sufferings of our Lord. He cried, "It is finished." The task is done. But when the Lord said that, he was still alive. Remember, this is the sixth saying. It is not until the seventh saying that the Lord dismissed his spirit, that he bowed his head and physically died. There is something over and beyond in the death of Christ for our sins that we hardly realize.

In Isaiah 53 there is a verse of profound meaning. Christ paid for our sins far more than just the physical pouring out of his blood upon the earth. "[The Lord God] shall see the travail of his soul, and shall be satisfied" (Isa. 53:11). Atonement is the satisfaction of God in the payment of the debt that we owe, and the prophet said that "[God] shall see the travail of his soul, and shall be satisfied." Our sins were paid for, atoned for, expiated, removed, washed away, taken away, dismissed from God's memory and sight forever—not only by the death of our Lord in the pouring out of his blood. Our atonement was also in the suffering of our Christ in his soul, in his heart. I do not know what that means; nor can finite mind enter into the suffering that must have been felt by the soul of the Son of God.

In Gethsemane when Jesus prayed, so great was his agony of spirit that his sweat seemed great drops of blood falling down to the ground. On the cross the Lord did not die from the wounds in his hands and his feet; nor did he die from the thrust of that iron spear into his heart. Jesus was already dead when the soldiers came and tore open his body. When the Roman spear pierced his heart, blood (red corpuscles) and limpid serum (water) flowed out. Christ died of a ruptured heart. The serum had already separated from the red corpuscles; and when the sac was punctured, blood and water flowed out. The Lord died of a broken heart. His Spirit was crushed; his soul was in agony. That is why he cried, "My God, my God, why hast thou forsaken me?" (Mark 15:34).

In the agony of that moment and hour, Jesus became sin. In his travail, in his suffering, and in his agony, his heart broke. Christ paid the penalty for our sins in his spirit, in his soul. "[Thou] shall see of the travail of his soul, and shall be satisfied." After the great atonement was made and the Lord cried, "It is finished," he bowed his head and dismissed his spirit into the hands of God. There was no doubt but that he was physically dead.

The Way to Heaven

What is finished? Not only our atonement and our salvation. The way into heaven, the door into glory, was opened wide through the death of the Son of God. All we do now is just walk in.

A pastor explained to a teenager who had leukemia, and who was lost, how to be saved. The boy broke in and said to the pastor, "Sir, is it that easy?" The pastor replied, "Son, it is easy for you, but it was not for him."

I can remember well the dramatic moment in the last World War when the prisoners of Corregidor and Bataan were liberated. When that dramatic and awesome moment of freedom came, it was very simple. A man cried, saying, "The Yanks are here!" and he cut the barbed wire. Those soldiers who were imprisoned to die walked out to freedom; they simply walked out. But if any of you remember World War II, can you ever forget the cost and the price before that barbed wire was torn apart and before those men could walk out?

There was the awesome cost at Guadalcanal. There were the battles in the Marshall Islands, in the Caroline Islands, and finally in Okinawa and Iwo Jima. There was the pouring out of blood into the Pacific Ocean as our brave men fought from island to island and from base to base until finally they came to the Philippines. It was a simple thing for the prisoners of Corregidor and Bataan just to walk out; but the price of their liberty was bought by the blood of thousands and thousands of American men.

The same is true with our salvation. It is easy for us. We just accept the gift; we just trust the Lord for it. We just take it and receive it. But he paid an infinite price for it. "[Thou] shall see the travail of his soul, and shall be satisfied." What a rich ransom!

The death of the Son of God, dying in his spirit and dying in his physical frame, brings to us a forever gift. It never needs to be repeated. As the author of Hebrews so gloriously wrote: "And as it is appointed unto men once to die, but after this the judgment: So Christ was once offered to bear the sins of many; and unto them that look for him shall he appear the second time without sin unto salvation" (Heb. 9:27–28).

We are to die one time, to be judged one time; and Christ made an atonement for our sins one time. It is a forever gift. It is a forever salvation. When we accept the Lord it is done forever and forever. As the author of the Hebrews wrote: "Wherefore he is able also to save them to the uttermost that come unto God by him, seeing he ever liveth to make intercession for them" (Heb. 7:25). Not only did Christ die for us, but he lives an intercessory life for us in order that some day, some glorious day, we shall appear with him in glory apart from sin.

Paul wrote: "For I know whom I have believed, and am persuaded that he is able to keep that which I have committed unto him against that day" (2 Tim. 1:12). Now, tomorrow, in old age, in the hour of death, standing at the judgment bar of God, and whatever aeons of eternity that lie beyond, the atonement that bought our salvation is a forever gift. "It is finished."

Salvation is for us to accept in his grace, in his love, in his mercy. We are just to take it. We all are included in the invitation. We are in the family of God; we are enrolled; we are in heaven; we are in his love and grace just by walking in, just by accepting. "It is finished!"

19
The Cross and the Crown

Then Pilate entered into the judgment hall again, and called Jesus, and said unto him, "Art thou the King of the Jews?"

Jesus answered him, "Sayest thou this thing of thyself, or did others tell it thee of me?"

Pilate answered, "Am I a Jew? Thine own nation and the chief priests have delivered thee unto me: what hast thou done?"

Jesus answered, "My kingdom is not of this world: if my kingdom were of this world, then would my servants fight, that I should not be delivered to the Jews: but now is my kingdom not from hence."

Pilate therefore said unto him, "Art thou a king then?" Jesus answered, "Thou sayest that I am a king. To this end was I born, and for this cause came I into the world, that I should bear witness unto the truth. Every one that is of the truth heareth my voice."

And it was the preparation of the passover, and about the sixth hour: and he saith unto the Jews, "Behold your King!"

But they cried out, "Away with him, away with him, crucify him." Pilate saith unto them, "Shall I crucify your King?" The chief priests answered, "We have no king but Caesar."

Then delivered he him therefore unto them to be crucified. And they took Jesus, and led him away.

And he bearing his cross went forth into a place called the place of a skull, which is called in the Hebrew Golgotha:

Where they crucified him, and two other with him, on either side one, and Jesus in the midst.

And Pilate wrote a title, and put it on the cross. And the writing was JESUS OF NAZARETH THE KING OF THE JEWS.

This title then read many of the Jews: for the place where Jesus was crucified was nigh to the city; and it was written in Hebrew, and Greek, and Latin.

Then said the chief priests of the Jews to Pilate, "Write not, The king of the Jews; but that he said, 'I am King of the Jews.' "

Pilate answered, "What I have written I have written" (John 18:33–37; 19:14–22).

The superscription that Pilate wrote above the cross of Christ was "Jesus of Nazareth, the King of the

Jews." He was so determined that all should read it that he wrote it in the language of all the people who might have been gathered there at that far-famed, much-attended Passover festival. He wrote the superscription in Hebrew, Greek, and Latin. When it was suggested to Pilate that he change the writing, Pilate said in determination and in final decision, "What I have written, I have written." So there it stands, the cross of our Lord and the superscription above it in those three languages.

Today there would be no cause and no reason to write that superscription in any language, for the language of the cross is universal. Just to see it is immediately to recognize it as the gospel of the grace of the Son of God.

One time I was in Oberammergau, seated with thousands of other people looking at the famous passion play. There were people present from the ends of the earth. Many of them were unable to understand German, but everyone listening and watching knew the language of the cross. Wherever the story is told of the dying Savior who is a king, there is intense interest. Even in the day of his crucifixion, the announcement of the reason for his death had to be written in three languages. Those three languages are symbols of so much.

The Language of the Cross

Pilate wrote the superscription in Hebrew, the language of religion. The Christian faith separates itself from all other religions in the earth. The unique feature of the Christian religion is this: It has Christ; the heart of it is Christ; the substance of it is Christ; the gospel is Christ. The Christian religion is not about him, an epic about him, or a philosophy about him. It is not anything except Jesus. The faith is Jesus Christ.

Jesus is the king and Lord of the human heart, of the human soul, of all judgment, and of the universe. Jesus is the great dissimilar and the great unlike.

Often I see books on the religions of the world, and on the front of the books are pictures of the religious leaders of the earth—Muhammad, Zoroaster, Confucius, Mahavira, Laotzu. Then, also, there will be a picture of the Lord Jesus. The book purports to give the story of the religious founders of the great faiths of time and of the present. When I see a thing like that I have a feeling that it is far more a violation of good taste than it is of spiritual judgment.

Jesus is just not to be placed in the same category as a philosopher like Socrates or a founder of religion like Muhammad. The difference between Muhammad and the Lord Jesus is the difference between night and day, between heaven and hell, between up and down, between the east and the west. The superscription was written in Hebrew, the language of faith and religion, "This is Jesus . . . King."

It was written in Greek, the language of culture and art. How very much the faith of our Lord has entered into the very framework, substance, foundation, and superstructure of western civilization. If one takes Jesus out of modern, civilized western life, it is a shambles. The great foundational truths upon which western civilization has been built are found in the faith of Jesus Christ. That is true in art, in poetry, in song, and in literature. It is true in every expression of western civilization.

"He is . . . King" was written not only in Hebrew, the language of faith, and not only in Greek, the language of civilization, of art, of literature; but it was also written in Latin, the language of statutes and government. The Sermon on the Mount, with its high ethical content, preached by the Lord Jesus, is the model of every truly great government of law in the earth. The sermon is civic, legal sublimity itself.

Our Lord even on the cross is raised up as a king. So avowed the superscription. "Jesus of Nazareth the King of the Jews" was written in Latin, in Greek, and in Hebrew. That is the prelude to the glorious, incomparable, marvelous exaltation of our Savior. Just as surely as God lives, just so surely will the Lord Jesus be crowned king of the universe.

There is nothing in theology that shall ever go beyond in truth and in fact the marvelous kinetic passage of the apostle Paul, written in the second chapter of the book of Philippians: "And being found in fashion as a man, he humbled himself, and became obedient unto death, even the death of the cross.

"Wherefore God also hath highly exalted him, and given him a name which is above every name:

"That at the name of Jesus every knee should bow, of things in heaven, and things in earth, and things under the earth;

"And that every tongue should confess that Jesus Christ is Lord, to the glory of God the Father" (Phil. 2:8–11).

To the praise and glory of God, Jesus is forever and universally *the* king. Hebrews 12:2 says, "Looking unto Jesus the author and finisher of our faith; who for the joy that was set before him endured the cross, despising the shame, and is set down at the right hand of the throne of God." This is King Jesus dying on the cross, exalted to the right hand of God, and the universal king of all creation.

The Figure of Truth Through the Ages

In the truth of that message on the cross of the kingship of our Lord Jesus, the ages and the centuries do confirm the mighty grace and glorious power of the cross and the crown. The spirit and the message of the king crucified, raised, and exalted now shapes government, art, and faith through all following history.

The superscription was written in Latin, the language of government. In the cross of Christ, in the obedience and suffering of our Lord, we find the great key to universal government and to universal peace.

I can well remember the first World War, which left the nation of Germany in a shambles. It would be hard for us to realize the depth of humiliation; the destruction; the awesome burden of payment, of neglect, and of the despicable, contemptuous attitude that the civilized world developed toward the German people. It generated in the national life of the German people a bitterness toward the entire world. That bitterness can be symbolized in a stone statue that the German people erected on the Polish frontier.

The statue was of a woman brooding in determination facing the Polish nation. Underneath that woman were these words inscribed: "Never forget, Germans, of what blind hatred has robbed you. Bide the hour that shall expiate the shame of this bleeding frontier." Then below were listed the names of the towns that once belonged to Prussia, the eastern German province, and that then and now belonged to Poland. In that bitterness, hatred, and malice placed there in brooding stone, there arose the seedbed in which the spirit of Hitler grew and grew. Finally it possessed the entire soul of the Germanic nation. There followed the indescribable atrocities, bloodshed, and maelstrom of war, fury, and death of World War II.

In contrast, some of you have flown over the great Andes Mountains that separate Chile from Argentina. On the main air route over the Andes the pilot will be careful to point out the Christ of the Andes. On one of the great high mountains in that marvelous, supernal range there is a vast statue of the living Christ and the cross. After years of warfare between Argentina and Chile, on the borderline between those nations the commonwealth of the two countries built that cross and the statue of Christ. This is the inscription on the base of the statue: "Sooner shall these mountains crumble into dust, than Argentina and Chile shall break the peace they have pledged at the foot of Christ our Redeemer."

Yes, the superscription on the cross was written in Latin, the language of government, "[This is] Jesus of Nazareth the King." All true government is based upon that spirit of sacrifice, love, and the pouring out of life.

Also, the shadow of that truth has fallen across the entire cultural and artistic world. He is declared a king in Greek. What a difference does the Spirit of Christ make in the art forms and in the literary and musical expressions of the world!

For example, if one were in Florence, Italy, doubtless he would visit the monastery of St. Mark's. I wanted to go there mostly because Savonarola, the flaming and marvelous preacher, the pre-Reformation messenger of God, was a monk in St. Mark's monastery. It was from the little cell in which he lived in that monastery that he made his way to the great duomo (the cathedral) and preached the gospel of the power and the saving efficacy of the name of Christ our Lord.

The little cells where the monks lived in St. Mark's monastery are unbelievable. The cells (little rooms) are covered with heavenly pictures, beautiful pictures, marvelous pictures. Some of the finest demonstrations of art on the earth are on the wooden walls of those monastery rooms. What does it mean? The meaning is patent and evident. As the monk lived there in that cell, as he prayed to God, and as he read the Holy

Scriptures, his mind and soul were elevated. Of an artistic temperament, he drew pictures of the dreams of his heart and of the visions of his soul. The pictures are of angels, of the celestial hope, of heaven, and of the glory of God. As one walks around and looks, he cannot help being impressed with the mind and the heart of those godly, consecrated men who dreamed such dreams, who saw such visions, and who painted such marvelous forms of art.

That is true in music. Some of the sublimest music was written by men who loved God and worshiped Christ.

Remove the influence of our Lord, and look at the sordid art forms that we find today on the stage, in the movie houses, and in the salacious novels—the unspeakable trash and filth that pass for modern literature. The superscription was written in Greek, in the language of art. Wherever there is kingship, nobility, exaltation, and heavenliness, there will one find the cross of Christ and the shadow of our Lord, King Jesus, reigning over the arts, the literature, and the music of the earth.

Last, the superscription was written in Hebrew, the universal language of faith. The shadow of the true godly commitment falls over the human heart and the human soul. If we suffer with him we shall also reign with him. Our Lord's invitation is to come, to take up the cross, to follow him, to die to self that we might live unto God. In dying to self there is a part that grief plays in our lives. Sorrow tempers us, strengthens us, and gives us courage. There is a part that trouble and tears play in the life that is crucified. Disappointment and frustration find a part in the crucified life.

There is a place that failure will play in our lives in the shadow of the cross. In how many ways did the Lord Jesus fail, utterly, abjectly, completely, and disastrously? He failed with the rich young ruler. He failed with the leaders of his day. He failed with his own people and his nation. In fact, if one were sardonic and unbelieving, he could point to the life of our Lord as an example of failure. But he is a king. In death he is a king, in suffering he is still a king, and in execution he is a king. For that is the way that we as Christians are to live. First the cross and then the crown.

This is Jesus, a king, and the shadow of that truth falls over all of human life. If we would reign with him, we must suffer with him. If we would live with him, we must die with him. If we would inherit the kingdom with him, we must be crucified with him. The cross and then the crown. This is Jesus the King.

All hail the pow'r of Jesus' name!
Let angels prostrate fall;
Bring forth the royal diadem,
And crown him Lord of all.

Let ev'ry kindred, ev'ry tribe,
On this terrestrial ball,
To him all majesty ascribe,
And crown him Lord of all.[3]

Notes

CHAPTER 1

1. Words by S. J. Henderson.
2. Words by Augustus Toplady.

CHAPTER 5

1. Words by William A. Ogden.
2. Words by George W. Robinson.

CHAPTER 7

1. © Homer A. Rodeheaver; international copyright secured. Used by permission.
2. Words by Joseph Scriven.

CHAPTER 8

1. Words by Elisha A. Hoffman.
2. Words by Isaac Watts.
3. Words by Isaac Watts.
4. Words by Robert Lowry.
5. John McCrae, "In Flanders Fields."

CHAPTER 9

1. Traditional Negro spiritual. Words adapted by John J. Work and Frederic J. Work.
2. Words by William Cowper.

CHAPTER 10

1. Words by Robert Lowry.

CHAPTER 19

1. Words to first stanza by Edward Perronet. Words to following stanza by John Rippon.